SCHOOL OF DISCIPLESHIP

A Kingdom Academy resource
www.kingdomacademy.org.uk

©Simon Rennie

First edition 2024

No part of this publication may be reproduced, stored in a retrieval system, or transmitted in any form or by any means - electronic, mechanical, photocopy, recording, or any others without the prior permission of the author. The only exception is brief quotations in printed reviews.

Scripture is taken, unless stated otherwise, from the HOLY BIBLE, NEW INTERNATIONAL VERSION. Copyright © 1973, 1978, 1984 International Bible Society.

Printed by Kindle Direct Publishing

So then, just as you received Christ Jesus as Lord,
continue to live your lives in him, rooted and built up in him,
strengthened in the faith as you were taught, and overflowing
with thankfulness.
Colossians 2:6-7

Dedication

My dedication is found in the closing pages of this book under the heading, *Final Remarks*, as I seek to remember and name the many people and organisations that shaped, nurtured and stretched my Christian discipleship.

Yet also an *Opening Remark,* a special written 'shout-out' to Becki for all her work that made this project possible – thank *you!*

School of Discipleship

Simon Rennie

Contents

CHAPTER 0	Back to School	11
CHAPTER 1	Let's Meet God	23
CHAPTER 2	Grace Love and Fellowship...	41
CHAPTER 3	Keep in Step	59
CHAPTER 4	Body Soul and Spirit	79
CHAPTER 5	Becoming More Jesus	105
CHAPTER 6	Thanksgiving	125
CHAPTER 7	Gifts Gifts Gifts	133
APPENDIX A	Prayer Praise and Prophecy	145
APPENDIX B	Read the Bible	154
APPENDIX C	Time With God	168
APPENDIX D	Solitude Simplicity and Submission ...	183
FINAL REMARKS		195

SCHOOL OF DISCIPLESHIP

Psalm 1:1-3

1 Blessed is the one
    who does not walk in step with the wicked
or stand in the way that sinners take
    or sit in the company of mockers,
2 but whose delight is in the law of the Lord,
    and who meditates on his law day and night.
3 That person is like a tree planted by streams of water,
    which yields its fruit in season
and whose leaf does not wither –
    whatever they do prospers.

CHAPTER 0

Back to School

For me, discipleship started as a process of trial and error. There were weekly sermons and even the midweek Bible study, but they felt disconnected. Attendance seemed more important than content. My church life started when I was still at school, and although some environments resembled school, there was never any homework. I was glad of that – of course. But still, how was this ignorant teenager going to grow as a Christian?

Information is not the same as formation. They say this present generation is the most informed generation. Our phones give us access to a wealth of knowledge. However, it doesn't necessarily make us wiser, able to make good choices, or even guarantee a level of common sense. I can learn about Christianity, and with that information, I can become a functional believer – but does that make me a disciple? Jesus wanted His disciples to make other disciples[1]. Over the years I've concluded that *making a disciple* isn't a weekend hobby or finding an hour or so in the week to do some 'Christian stuff', it's not even about grabbing eight minutes at the start of the day to ease my conscience by remembering God. Discipleship isn't a lesson or a programme – it's an entire life.

There are already bookshelves full of discipleship manuals in all shapes and sizes. So, why another? This volume is deliberately different. Over forty years of being a Christian, and over thirty years of being a church minister, I'm going to be unpacking my own spiritual journey to discover key biblical perspectives to nurture effective Christian discipleship.

First the structure, this book consists of two distinct sections, the numbered chapters (1-7) and the appendices (A-D). It's an attempt to separate out the basic Christian disciplines, such as prayer and Bible reading, from the more relational and spiritual components of nurturing a God-centred life.

I'm no good at do-it-yourself. I can go to these home improvement stores and be overwhelmed by all the tools and equipment there is on offer. Having the tools, doesn't mean you know how to use them. From experience, many believers can operate their Bible, say a prayer, and attend a local church, yet they've never really been told what these tools and resources are for, and how they can be used effectively for the job we're called to do.

---

[1] Matthew 28:19-20

BACK TO SCHOOL

If you were sold Christianity as a 'ticket to heaven', then you've come into His presence believing in something more akin to our selfish nature, than God's lavish plans and purposes. Don't worry, I'm not going to take away your assurance of eternal life. Without a doubt *life* is what Jesus came to bring, and life in abundance[2]. It's the selfishness and individualism so prevalent in our society that needs to be weeded out from our Christian mindset, otherwise discipleship won't make sense and the benefits of Kingdom living will be completely missed.

> The most significant part of your personal testimony is not what you've been **saved out of**, but what you've been **saved into**.

Christianity is not all about the final destination, but the life-changing responsibilities we have on the journey. The most significant part of your personal testimony is not what you've been *saved out of*, but what you've been *saved into*. Understanding that, will equip you with spiritual tools that will both help you, and rescue and heal others.

Welcome to my **School of Discipleship**. It's mine, amid hundreds of other publications, but this actual book (hopefully) is yours, so use it as you like. Get some highlighter pens, underline stuff, circle words, fold the

---

[2] John 3:16, 10:10 & 14:6

SCHOOL OF DISCIPLESHIP

page edges down, whatever works to help in your maturing. You're the disciple, and God has so much for you to discover and enjoy.

Let's start with a definition. The word disciple (*mathētés*) means student or pupil. Though within this textbook definition we need to allow for the historical setting of the Bible. The ancient Hebraic culture saw knowledge as primarily gained through experience, rather than in a classroom setting. Therefore, a more accurate English translation for a New Testament disciple would be, *apprentice.* In the UK educational system an apprentice learns a particular set of skills, with an emphasis of hands-on experience, which will help lead to specific areas of future employment. Such as, a carpenter, a plumber, a decorator, or a hairstylist. Traditionally in the West, those students deemed more academically able were encouraged to go to university, where their core subject was not necessarily job-orientated, and where their learning environments were primarily lecture rooms and libraries. These two modern approaches to education, the apprentice and the undergraduate, model the main difference between Hebraic and Greco-Roman thinking, that still influences most of the world's schools and universities today.

In the Gospels, Jesus was referred to as a rabbi[3], and like other rabbis, He had disciples[4] and modelled a learning environment typical of the era and culture. The focus of Christ's ministry was the Kingdom of God.

---

[3] John 3:2 & 20:16.
[4] This wasn't unique to Jesus, some of his first disciples had been followers of John the Baptist. John 1:35-38 records an event when two disciples transfer their rabbinic allegiance. John isn't perturbed, in John 3:26-30, he concludes, *'He must become greater; I must become less'*

BACK TO SCHOOL

Through proclamation, He announced the message of the Kingdom[5]. Through transformation (healings and deliverance), He demonstrated the power of the Kingdom[6]. Through compassion, social inclusion, forgiveness and personal restoration, He showed the ethics of the Kingdom[7]. In brief, Jesus's teachings were accompanied with practical expressions of His ethics and divine power, a task He then empowers His disciples to do[8]. Genuine Christian discipleship did not take the form of a teaching series presented within the four walls of a room, it was authentically *everyday* in its practice, touching and influencing culture and lifestyle choices.

I can't be too scathing about the UK church, having been a minister and church leader in various settings for over thirty years. However, overall, our Sunday worship gatherings look like a lecture theatre, with rows of chairs focussed on a single point on a slightly raised stage. Though far more annoyingly to me, is that our smaller midweek groups tend toward modelling a classroom culture too. So, a reasonable question to ask, without seeking to be overly critical, would be,

> *Has our approach to discipleship effectively equipped our congregants in the power of God, to heal the sick and cast out demons?*

---

[5] Matthew 13. The majority of Jesus's parables were about the Kingdom of God.
[6] Luke 11:20
[7] Like 4:18. Jesus tended to give time to those on the margins of society, the poor (Luke 14:13), the lepers (Luke 11:13), tax-collectors (Luke 19:5) and those deemed 'sinners' (Matthew 9:10).
[8] Luke 9:1-2

SCHOOL OF DISCIPLESHIP

In fairness, we could start with a much easier ice-breaker question.

How were you discipled?

Does your present church disciple its congregants? If so, how and how is that measured or evaluated?

Evaluated? Are you wanting us all to sit a Scripture exam?

No. Well... possibly an online multiple-choice quiz might not be an entire waste of time. However, I was thinking more about Luke 10, when Jesus sent out the seventy(-two)[9] to model Kingdom ministry, including healing and proclaiming, or at least *explaining* the good news of the Kingdom[10].

Back to school. I studied mathematics as a senior student, a subject which was traditionally split into *pure* and *applied*. We even had two different teachers for the different disciplines. I'd like to argue that biblical Christianity only has an *applied* component. Sure, there are libraries all over the Western world filled with the *pure* aspect of Christianity. Books, journals and doctrinal papers containing the ancient and continuing musings of theologians and Christian philosophers. Nevertheless, having sat in such a library for three years gaining my degree, I can tell you, hand on heart, my personal discipleship grew more through one week's mission in south London as an ignorant eighteen-year-old[11], than it ever did as a twentysomething under- and post-graduate. I'm grateful for my theological education. I learnt a lot!

---

[9] Just a nod to the fact that some New Testament manuscripts have *seventy* and others, *seventy-two*.
[10] Luke 10:8-9
[11] More on this adventure later in the book.

BACK TO SCHOOL

But only a handful of lecturers were willing (or able) to join the dots to apply the academic to the everyday. On reflection it was a discipline I chose to do myself, to give my studies increased value and integrity. Sadly, not all my co-students chose that path, and their first zeal for Christ seemed to get lost among the Ancient Near Eastern texts, the complex linguistics of New Testament hermeneutics, and the opposing unresolved doctrines of the European Reformers. Again, I am grateful for the studious thinkers, the historians and linguists who have done the heavy spade work, over the centuries, to help unpack and bring insights to God's words. Though more especially those gifted theologians who can apply their rich findings to help equip the local church in her Jesus-centred mission.

Staying with the theme of school and education, later in my ministry, I needed to gain a recognisable qualification in teaching adults, in order to legitimately teach an accredited Bible course, that I'd actually written! One of the things I learnt was around creating lesson plans, and the rather obvious need to state your learning outcomes. This consisted of a simple and concise paragraph, or a few bullet-points, to clearly announce the purpose of the lesson and your expected goals, i.e. *the learning outcomes*. Since then, I've often wondered how different church would be, especially midweek small groups, if the facilitator, had (at least in their own head) some thought through, predetermined, learning outcomes. So, in recognition of the title of this book (**School of Discipleship**), I have decided to start every subsequent chapter with a *learning outcomes* paragraph.

Another component to aid learning, popular in Western schools, is *homework*. Often a focussed piece of work to help the student consolidate the learning outcomes of the previous lesson. Which brings us back to one of Christ's final statements to His closest disciples. Their mission (homework), if they chose to accept it, was to go and make disciples. How? Well, Jesus was quite clear, it was a threefold plan[12].

Firstly, to go into all the world. Therefore, to make these new disciples, the present disciples would have to engage with unbelievers, those presently ignorant of the Good News message. Jesus reworded this in Acts 1, where He explained that their mission field was to be Jerusalem, Judea, Samaria and then – the rest of the world[13]. It's helpful (and legitimate) to think of these regions not only as defined geographies, but as different demographics. Jerusalem, your own people, the place where you live or work. Judea, again people of a similar culture, though perhaps you might be thinking those rural yokels aren't quite as sophisticated as us city-folk. Samaria, that's difficult, a lot in common, but historically hostile; wisdom and courage is required to reach these people. Then the rest of the world – well who knows what people groups, cultures and weird languages we'll discover out there?

Secondly, baptise the new believers. Space is short here to explain fully, however, salvation and baptism in the New Testament seemed intrinsically linked. So first we evangelise, sometimes cross-culturally, but always with the explicit expectation to see new converts and to acknowledge their newfound faith through baptism.

---

[12] Matthew 28:19-20
[13] Acts 1:8b

BACK TO SCHOOL

Finally, and thirdly, to teach these new disciples everything Christ has taught you. The teaching component within discipleship is explicit here – everything Jesus has shared, especially as we have it recorded in the Gospel accounts. We can expand this, because we know that some of Paul's letters and the epistle of James were circulating within the early church before any of the Gospels had been written. So, a little common sense and application means we don't exclusively teach from the Gospels, but like Paul and Jesus, and indeed, John the Baptist, and extensively the writer of Hebrews, we need to use the Old Testament to help build the case that the historical Jesus of Nazareth was indeed the promised Messiah[14], and to explain the numerous consequences for life and worship that those eternal truths release.

Now, having mentioned 'life and worship' we come to a third component of early church discipleship teaching. Let's quickly recap, first, Jesus, and everything He taught and did. Second, a growing context to grasp the implications of Jesus being both Christ and Lord[15]. And thirdly, all manner of practical matters surrounding our ongoing behaviour.

---

[14] The Book of Hebrews seems deliberately designed to show the superior work of Jesus (over angels, over Moses, over the Law) leading to His *once and for all* sacrifice for the atonement of sin. Paul painstakingly does the same in Galatians and Romans. John the Baptist uses Isaiah 40 as his preaching text (Matthew 3:3), and Jesus references the Old Testament throughout His ministry to explain His teachings and purposes. Matthew 5-7 would be an example. as would Luke 4:17-21 (the Nazareth manifesto) and Mark 11-13 (*Passion* week, drenched in Old Testament imagery and prophetic fulfilments.)

[15] Acts 2:36, or *Lord and Messiah* (the Hebrew version of *Christ*). We often think of Acts 2 as *tongues of fire* (2:3), the Holy Spirit, and a time of mass conversion (2:41, *three thousand*). Peter's anointed sermon is not an easy read for most of us, as it's framed within a number of Old Testament concepts – but it worked!

SCHOOL OF DISCIPLESHIP

Jesus nails this in Matthew 5-7, often called, *The Sermon on the Mount*. We'll look at this in more detail later in the book. However, these three chapters are packed with practical advice, encouragements and challenges.

In Paul's letters, we can detect this early church teaching model. He often starts by celebrating our faith in Christ, our spiritual inheritance, Christ rescuing us from darkness into light. On occasion he draws on the Old Testament to support his case for Christ, or even a new song that's doing the rounds[16]. Christ's sacrificial life, is clearly an example for us to follow, leading to a further section on moral behaviour. A radically different lifestyle, no more gossip, slander, gluttony, and sexual immorality[17], to help us better pursue Christ, our calling, the Holy Spirit, learning the power of prayer, the value of generosity and the need to support (spiritually and materially) other churches and ministries[18].

It's a lot! However, because discipleship is in the everyday, being increasingly Christlike will become second nature. Or, quite literally, the restored nature of our new creation identity[19].

Our task, like those before us, is to make disciple-making disciples. That is, just as Jesus did, to help form disciples that are able to make and disciple others.

---

[16] The opening chapter of Ephesians and Colossians show this, along with texts that are very likely based on, or at least acknowledging, a new Christian hymn. Philippians 2:6-11, Colossians 1:15-20 and 1 Timothy 3:16b.
[17] Various lists appear, Galatians 5:19-21, Ephesians 5:3-7, and Colossians 3:5-17.
[18] Ephesians 5 & 6 and Philippians 4 follow this model.
[19] 2 Corinthians 5:17

BACK TO SCHOOL

Are you ready to enrol in the **School of Discipleship**? It may well take you out of your comfort zone – I hope it does. It may well even take you to the ends of the Earth. I know many friends who have upped sticks and gone on Holy Spirit inspired adventures. Such a word was prayed over my Colombian wife at her baptism. At that point she'd never left the country, with the only exception of a short trip to Panama, where she amazingly heard Billy Graham preach the Gospel, the night she gave her heart to Jesus. Over ten years later she was in England, then later still we met, and within six years of being married, we had ministered in eight different countries, on three different continents.

Following Jesus is *still* an adventure.

Oh, and before we finish – the homework. I nearly forgot.

So, here it is,

> *In addition to 'love', which two other words would you use to best describe God?*

Go on, have a little think about that. To remind you again, your homework is,

> *In addition to 'love', which two other words, describing God, have helped you in your discipleship?*

Did you see what I did there? In attempting to repeat the question, I changed it a bit. But don't panic. Don't lose sleep over this, I'll let you mark your own work. Have a think and I'll see you at the beginning of chapter 1.

Psalm 34:8

Taste and see that the Lord is good; blessed is the one who takes refuge in him.

CHAPTER 1

Let's Meet God

LEARNING OUTCOME | To discover two aspects of God's character that will be effective in our ongoing discipleship.

> *Note to reader, that's far from being the most explanative learning outcome, but I don't want to give too much away about the coming contents of this chapter.*

In John 14, Jesus states if you've seen Him, you've seen the Father[20], and just before that Jesus explained that He was the only way to the Father[21]. I once had a physical Bible (as opposed to an app on my phone), where I was shown that on every double-page spread of John's Gospel, the word *Father* was present. The original Eden relationship we had with God was seriously damaged, and the Godhead[22] is working together on a

---

[20] John 14:9
[21] John 14:6
[22] The title used when wanting to refer to all three persons of the Trinity.

mission to restore what was lost. We see the presence of the Godhead at the beginning of Christ's public ministry, Jesus's baptism, the Spirit's anointing and the Father's affirmation[23]. In John 3:16, the motivation for this mission is made explicit – love.

> For God so loved the world that he gave his one and only Son, that whoever believes in him shall not perish but have eternal life. **John 3:16**

God's great love for His world leads to a series of extraordinary, costly and sacrificial events for our salvation and restoration. So back to the homework from the last chapter. In addition to the obvious word, *love*, which two other words would you use to describe God?

Or, which two words that describe God, in addition to *love*, motivate and shape your daily discipleship?

Perhaps *holiness*? It's hard to ignore such a clear suggestion from heaven.

> Each of the four living creatures had six wings and was covered with eyes all round, even under its wings. Day and night they never stop saying:
> '"Holy, holy, holy is the Lord God Almighty," who was, and is, and is to come.'
> **Revelation 4:8**

We must never take for granted or play down the holiness of God. The celestial realm rarely sings about anything else. However, is

---

[23] Matthew 3:16-17

this continual and repetitive worship song from Revelation 4 simply about God's holiness? Clearly from the passage, it's also about God's unchanging nature. Is true worship a form of escapism, as we celebrate a holy unchanging God in a world that is far from holy and forever changing? Perhaps there's a clue in the book's title – Revelation?

You might come from a church where, much to your annoyance, the same simple song is repeated again and again. Why? You ask. The words haven't changed, nor has the tune! Why do we need to repeat it? There again, why do you continue to read your Bible year after year – the words haven't changed? Let's not forget, that when we read the most familiar of passages, God's living presence, can still bring the most surprising insights. The words are alive, they're inspired, which doesn't mean they're just great and awesome, it means they literally carry the breath of God[24]. The Bible may well at times be documenting historical facts, but those words remain alive and active; more than able to pierce your soul and cleanse your thoughts.

I like to think of the creatures worshipping God in Revelation 4, not so much repeating their simple song, but as they gaze upon the Eternal God, their revelation of God is forever changing, developing, being freshly inspired. The result, a further cry of, *holy, holy, holy*, which translates into modern speech as, *Wow! Did not see that before.*

Perhaps no one ever told you, but it's the reason we repeat songs, so that the implications of the words, which are often deliberately few and easy to understand, can *sink* into our soul and spirit. I'm

---

[24] 2 Timothy 3:16

not a fan of Formula 1 motor-racing. To me it looks tediously repetitive. And it is, those cars go round the exact same circuit over and over again. Yet it's a race, needing mental skill, physical endurance and motoring strategy. As the worship band repeat the same song for the fourth time, some of the congregation may well be bored, confused, annoyed, some give up and sit down. Others remain engaged, their hands rise up in an act of adoration that the words alone can't quite capture, some start to cry, others sense a remarkable and unexpected healing in their body, or in their mind, or in their spirit. God is holy and unchanging, and because of that He can still touch and order my messed-up life of angst and insecurities. In the physical realm we're all repeating the same words and reading the same Bible[25], yet in the spiritual realm some of us have been awakened to the God of yesterday *today*, discovering that His love endures forever. How can we capture such an amazing loving God in just two additional words?

In the twenty years I've asked this question to gap year students and conference delegates, I've never expected anyone to decide upon, *relational* and *revelatory*. Truth is, it probably took me at least twenty-five years to settle for these two words, and even then, I may well have stolen them from someone else.

Relational

God is relational. Alternative words can also capture this aspect of God's character, such as friendship and fellowship, that convey God to be personal and personally knowable. From the opening

---

[25] I'm not equating hymns and modern songs with the authority of Scripture. However, absolute truths remain absolute, so undiluted biblical truths whether on the page, in a sermon, or sung as a worship song contain the same revelatory power and life.

chapters of Genesis we see God interacting with humanity unlike any other part of His creation. He tells us to multiply[26]. Tangent warning! Hmm? Did he tell the other animals to do that? Or did He rely on their basic instincts? Why would God deliberately tell us to reproduce? Does the language of Genesis 1 suggest that human sexuality is different from non-human sexual activity? Anyway, moving on...

The first man was given a job, an administrative one (I hate admin) – naming the animals[27]. In Eden, God seemed to talk with the Man and the Woman[28] daily[29]. I may end up making too much of this, and it could have been purely functional in content as opposed to truly relational. God could have been turning up each day to ask if they'd done their chores. However, I would strongly suggest the evidence is there to deduce this was far more than a manager checking up on His employees. The narrative states, unlike the rest of creation, we were made in God's image, and later He placed His very breath within us[30]. I think God had deliberately made part of His creation in a way that He could truly *relate* to it, and I mean, far more than a cat owner cares for their pet!

Life can be best learnt from reflecting and chatting through experiences. I love the notion that God had a daily chat with humanity, in the form of a genuine friendship, and over time, this would naturally shape some sort of process for their personal development – was this God's intended model for discipleship?

---

[26] Genesis 1:28
[27] Genesis 2:19
[28] Eve received her name from Adam after the Fall, Genesis 3:20. Was this the now sinful corrupt Adam taking his job of naming the 'animals' to an extreme?!
[29] Genesis 3:8a
[30] Genesis 1:27 & 2:7

SCHOOL OF DISCIPLESHIP

It's completely unproven, I admit, but not altogether unbiblical. They say a little knowledge is a dangerous thing. Therefore, far better to hang out with the Creator, eating from the Tree of Life, with all the time in the world – literally – than to take a shortcut to knowledge with the fruit from the forbidden tree.

We tend to want to know things, not only, right from wrong, but clarity regarding the exact boundaries. Such a tendency leads to religion, an obsession with the letter of the law, as opposed to the spirit of the law. A petulant child, pushing their parent's buttons – to see what they can get away with. Or perhaps like Christian teenagers when discovering attraction to one another, wanting to know the boundaries in showing physical affection – how far is too far?

The apostle Paul admits the Law just made him feel a failure and a sinner[31] – so much for laws and the knowledge of good and evil.

First century rabbis spent extensive periods of time with their disciples, modelling an approach to teaching based on hands-on experiences and memorable storytelling. Information would be imparted through example and answering relevant and pressing questions. I think this form of discipleship is not only biblical, as modelled by Jesus, but could well be based on God's initial intentions for the original Eden project. Sadly, we love a shortcut. We sensibly load them onto our computer's desktop for speed and convenience. We might watch, via social media, various 'life hacks' to save time, to gain the upper hand, to improve our efficiency. You may even be reading this book to find a handy bullet-pointed list to instantly make you an effective disciple. To

---

[31] Romans 3:20

LET'S MEET GOD

an extent, I hope you are looking for some clues or an insightful hack to improve your walk with God. Nevertheless, I believe the key to following Jesus is the genuineness of our relationship with God, and like all relationships there are three fundamental foundations,

1. Communication
2. Communication
3. Communication

Call it prayer, call it praise, call it Bible meditation, and conversational ways of reading the Scriptures. In addition, it will also include meeting Christ through fellowshipping with other believers, and of course, the unique spiritual encounters we have by God's grace through the sacraments[32]. Even so, it all boils down to communication, different forms of communication, listening, sharing, laughing, weeping. Though most essentially, whatever the shape of communication, we're called to converse with the living God. When Jesus taught His disciples to pray, He told them they could address God as *Dad*[33] – that's relational!

Here's a quick reflection for you. If you have a daily personal devotion, sometimes called a 'quiet time', does it take the shape of a classroom study, or that of friends catching up? Remembering

---

[32] Most Protestant churches hold to two sacraments, baptism and the Lord's Supper. Though how they choose to observe them varies immensely. These commands (instructions) that came direct from Jesus (1 Corinthians 11:23-26 [this is the earliest written account which succinctly captures the memorial element of the Last Supper] & Matthew 28:19) are seen as physical means to understand God's grace. Baptism, God's gracious ability through Christ's death and resurrection to forgive. The Lord's Supper, again encourages us to reflect on the gracious gift of Christ's sacrifice.
[33] Matthew 6:9

the last chapter, do you default to your Greco-Roman mindset or are you developing a more Hebraic culture?

Need help in answering? Or even, understanding the question? In your personal devotions are you following a Bible programme, with set reading objectives? Are these personal devotions a regular length of time, 10 minutes, 20 minutes, or more? Are your prayers predominately petitions, or do you simply chat with God? If you're using a hardcopy paper-based physical Bible, have a quick think about its layout, is it simply the biblical text, or does it have study notes, information boxes, maps, and book outlines?

> When reading the Bible, we have constant real-time access to its Author. That's an absolute game-changer when it comes to reading the Bible

Please, don't get me wrong, all these Bible aids can be valuable. Nevertheless, on their own, they make the Bible into a study book. And as long as it looks like a textbook, like something you might have had at school, the more you'll resort to classroom thinking and behaviour. Consider this, the Bible is like extracts from God's private diary[34]. The Bible is rich in literature, including memorable

---

[34] John 21:25 supposes that if everything Jesus did was written down there wouldn't be enough room in the world for the books. Therefore, how many more planets would we need to house the *Complete Works of Yahweh*? Our

LET'S MEET GOD

anecdotes, timeless poetry, motivational stories, mysteries, insights and life-changing truths. Imagine for a moment these Scriptures are all there for your enjoyment and inspiration, rather than as a set text to study. I'll probably bang on about this throughout the book. I love Scripture. I honour its authority as the timeless and trustworthy Words of God. As I return to the same passage year after year, I still trust the Holy Spirit to show me more. Therefore, I'm not dissing the Bible, but I do question how some Christians use it, and if their methods and approaches are effective in enjoying and discovering its truths and its deliberately hidden treasures[35].

A common obstacle to our discipleship is a classroom mentality that makes us approach the Bible as an ancient text, with the assumption that the original authors are all dead. Well, those authors are dead, but not *the* Author. Pretty unique, eh? When reading the Bible, we have constant real-time access to its Author. That's an absolute game-changer when it comes to reading the Bible – and don't forget it.

Granted those last paragraphs may have been a bit of a tangent, and I'll return to accessing Scripture in a later chapter, but they do speak of relationship. As we lay some essential foundations for effective discipleship, one, is to avoid overly identifying with Western notions of study, that can so easily eclipse Christ's amazing invitation to be named among His friends[36].

Bibles are just a drop in the ocean, a God-ordained glimpse into some of His 'greatest hits'. Just a theory. We'll return to this later in the book.
[35] Proverbs 25:2 & Isaiah 45:3
[36] John 15:15

SCHOOL OF DISCIPLESHIP

God is relational. Salvation history (the linear narrative in the Bible that explains God's plan for restoration, forgiveness and a future hope) reveals God determined, at His own expense, to rescue and restore our tarnished image. This is not clinical. This is relational, sacrificial, costly and motivated by love.

Back in Genesis, our banishment from the garden did not lead to separation from God; as some evangelists love to preach, with illustrations of two opposing cliff tops, with a vast chasm between that can't naturally be bridged. In fact, at the time of Adam and Eve's expulsion from the garden, God went with them. If He hadn't the Bible would be a very short! Don't get me wrong, without a doubt the relationship was severely damaged, beyond human repair, and we lost our physical immortality, but God stood by us, helped us, clothed us[37], guided us, gave us promises (covenants) and repeatedly restored our catastrophes and gave us hints and pictures of a future hope[38]. By the time many of these promises are fulfilled, we find Jesus, the exact representation of the Father[39], and on the night, He was betrayed, He explicitly describes our relationship together as friends, not just functional servants.

> I no longer call you servants, because a servant does not know his master's business. Instead, I have called you friends, for everything that I learned from my Father I have made known to you. **John 15:15**

In Genesis 11 & 12 we discover God's plans for Abraham and Sarah, they were hoping to retire, yet God had family plans that would touch the entire world. In Exodus 3, Moses asks for

---

[37] Genesis 3:21
[38] That list is in part a brief synopsis of the entire Old Testament.
[39] Hebrews 1:3

LET'S MEET GOD

information about God. God describes Himself as the God of Abraham, Isaac and Jacob[40]. A God of real people. God *is* relational.

How we choose to describe God, often reveals our relationship (or lack of it) with God. I don't want to be too controversial so early on, but if you overly focus on a concept of holiness that separates you from God, then to a certain extent the value of the Cross is muted. It is within God's untarnished holiness, goodness and grace, that He invites us to enter the most holy of places, to dwell in His presence and to have the reality of the Holy Spirit make His home (temple) within us so He can reside in our lives[41]. Such language reminds me of John the Baptist being told to look for the one the Spirit remains upon[42], as believers that should be all of us. It's been suggested that in the Old Testament the Spirit came upon people, whereas in the New Testament the Spirit resides within us.

- Christmas: Immanuel, God with us
- Pentecost: Holy Spirit, God in us!

Whatever the amount of damage caused by the events in Genesis 3, the sacrifice of the Cross and the victory of the Empty Tomb have restored things; possibly even stronger than Eden, with God no longer a casual visitor, but a cohabiting presence – *blimey*, He's only gone and moved in!

Early on in my Christian walk, I heard the cliché,

---

[40] Exodus 3:14-15
[41] Hebrews 4:16, James 4:8 & 1 Corinthians 6:19
[42] John 1:33

SCHOOL OF DISCIPLESHIP

Christianity is not a religion, it's a relationship.

I understood the rhetoric, and it made for a good conversation opener with non-believers. Yet more, much more – it's true! That cliché is a life-changing, paradigm shifting, truth. By God's amazing grace, I have become God's friend.

Now read this,

> [21] that all of them [disciples] may be one, Father, just as you are in me [Jesus] and I am in you. May they also be in us so that the world may believe that you have sent me. [22] I have given them the glory that you gave me, **that they may be one as we are one** – [23] I in them and you in me – so that they may be brought to complete unity.
> **John 1:21-23 (with my emphasis)**

Just as we are one! Wow! I've never *fully* understood the workings of the Trinity, and now we've been adopted into it! So, how does that work?

Perhaps the answer to that last question is the very definition of discipleship.

Effective biblical discipleship doesn't begin with a series of lessons, memory verses, or a recommended reading list, it begins with God's truth and invitation to meet Him, Father, Son and Holy Spirit, in order for our original design and Eden factory settings to be restored.

LET'S MEET GOD

> And we all, who with unveiled faces contemplate[a] the Lord's glory, are being transformed into his image with ever-increasing glory, which comes from the Lord, who is the Spirit.
> **2 Corinthians 3:18**

God is a person, or more accurately, three persons in one, but what's important here is His personhood. He is not an object within His creation to be studied; or an element in that same universe to be observed. He is an emotive being, without beginning or end, choosing, in love, to engage with us. He invites us to draw close – what a privilege[43].

Revelatory

Admittedly not the obvious choice of words to describe God. Blame a theological education, but also my charismatic spirituality, that values the New Testament gift of prophecy.

God is a God of revelation. I'm not referencing here the last book of the Bible, but the whole of the Bible. In the Scriptures, God reveals Himself to us. Genesis 1:1, He's a creator God, in verse 26, God exists in some form of plurality. He has a purpose for humanity, He expects us to hold to His moral code. Where there is failure, He seeks to redeem and restore. His very names, of which He has plenty, reveal His character,

---

[43] James 4:8

SCHOOL OF DISCIPLESHIP

El Shaddai	The Lord God Almighty	Genesis 17:1
Jehovah[44] Jireh	The Lord Who Provides	Genesis 22:13-14
Jehovah Nissi	The Lord Our Banner	Exodus 17:15
Jehovah Shalom	The Lord is Peace	Judges 6:22-24
Jehovah Raab	The Lord My Shepherd	Psalm 23:1
Jehovah Rapha	The Lord Our Healer	many[45]
Jehovah Shammah	God is There	Ezekiel 48:35

This list is far from complete (seven felt like a good biblical number), and the Bible texts are generally the first time the name is used in the Hebrew text.

From the seven names I referenced, God is revealing His character, almighty, all-knowing. The provision was for Abraham's sacrifice, not financial in this context, but saving his son, Issac. Later the God who provides would provide His own Son. A banner of protection, like a computer firewall, the imagery is akin to a victorious army's standard or flag. Amid pressures and fears, our God is the God of peace, our Good Shepherd, as seen in Jesus (John 10:11), and our extensive holistic healer – again as demonstrated in Christ's ministry. Finally, the last revealed name of God in the Old Testament, is connected with a vision of a restored nation where

---

[44] Both Jehovah and Yahweh are different translations and transliterations of the Hebrew. Which to the Jews was so holy, they reduced God's name to an abbreviation – YWYH and used *Adonai,* which translates, Lord. In many English Bible translations where LORD is written in small caps, it's a translation from *Adonai.*

[45] 2 Kings 5:10 physical healing. Psalm 34:18 emotional healing. Daniel 4:34 serious mental healing. Psalm 103:2-3 spiritual healing.

LET'S MEET GOD

God dwells; first Christ dwells with us, and then the Holy Spirit dwells within us – *Jehovah Shammah*.

When we move to the New Testament, Jesus has too many names to mention. In John's Gospel alone, Jesus identified Himself using God's original 'I am' language from Exodus 3:14 and adding seven specific titles.

I am the bread of life	John 6:35
I am the light of the world	John 8:12
I am the gate	John 10:9
I am the good shepherd	John 10:14-15
I am the resurrection and the life	John 11:25-26
I am the way the truth and the life	John 14:6
I am the true vine	John 15:1-2

All these descriptions *reveal* an aspect of Christ, His character, His purpose, and His ministry.

It could be argued that the only things we know about God, are those that He has first chosen to reveal to us.

For a person to develop, they need at least one relationship where they can be totally honest, a place where they can disclose information about themselves, and are willing to receive feedback from one other or more. God is in the habit of disclosing information, and generally that information makes Him accessible and knowable – relational.

Interestingly, God's revelations, surprisingly, unlike so much 'christian' fodder on the internet, do not involve an accurate timeline about the end times, the rise of a One World order, or a historical list of Papal figures and their apostasies. Though, healthily and thankfully, His revelations are explicit concerning His love for us, rich in grace and mercy, including His willingness to forgive, redeem, restore, empower, and equip us for all sorts of Kingdom work and opportunities. There's adoption into His family, the anointing to carry His Glory and the promise of His unending personal presence[46].

For God to be relational, He still needs to operate in revelation. Obviously, we have the Bible – a massive volume of God's revelations and interactions with His creation. It is from the Bible that we know God longs to bless us[47], number our hairs[48], give us guidance[49]. He hasn't changed. God wants to give us personal insights, serving as confirmations of His ongoing loving presence. Such personal prophecies, 'words' or pictures don't rewrite Scripture, indeed they shouldn't, for it's the certainty of fixed Scripture that helps us to identify the genuineness from the dross.

---

[46] Too many to mention, but here goes, John 3:16, Galatians 2:20, Ephesians 2:4, James 2:13, 1 John 1:9, Ephesians 4:12 & 2:10, Romans 8:15, John 17:22-23 and Matthew 28:20b
[47] Luke 13:34, even in our sin and distress.
[48] Luke 12:7
[49] Acts 16:7-9

LET'S MEET GOD

Here the Bible and the Holy Spirit work hand in hand again,[50] to mature our relationship with God. We're not students. We're friends. The God who lavishes His love upon us is both relational and revelatory - that's important to grasp to help us grow as a true disciple.

---

[50] *Again*, in the sense that all Scripture is already the work of the Spirit (2 Timothy 3:16) and that prophecy (a gift of the Spirit) is required to be weighed, by Truth (1 John 4:6 and 1 Thessalonians 5:20).

2 Corinthians 13:14

May the grace of the Lord Jesus Christ, and the love of God, the fellowship of the Holy Spirit be with you all.

CHAPTER 2

Grace Love and Fellowship

LEARNING OUTCOME | To discover a spiritual journey of discipleship that begins with grace, so that no one can feel disqualified, and involves genuine fellowship and friendship with God.

In asking you to think of two additional words to describe God, I assumed that 'love' was a given starting place. Why?

God's motivation is made explicit in John 3:16, and one of earliest Scriptures we have where God chooses to reveal His nature.

> Then the LORD came down in the cloud and stood there with him and proclaimed his name, the LORD. **6** And he passed in front of Moses, proclaiming, 'The LORD, the LORD, the compassionate and gracious God, slow to anger, abounding in

> love and faithfulness, **⁷** maintaining love to thousands, and forgiving wickedness, rebellion and sin.
> **Exodus 34:5-7a**[51]

In addition, the last verse of 2 Corinthians remains a helpful place to start. It's trinitarian in its understanding of God. It gives Jesus, His extensive threefold title. Yet my favourite aspect of the verse, is that it serves to map out a journey of discipleship, crucial and essential for every believer.

> May the grace of the Lord Jesus Christ, and the love of God, the fellowship of the Holy Spirit be with you all.
> **2 Corinthians 13:14**

Before we map out the discipleship journey, let's do some background work around the text and start to discover the full extent of this single sentence prayer, and why *love* is an essential

---

[51] In Exodus 34:7, the verse ends with God stating He doesn't let the guilty go unpunished, even to the third and fourth generation. God has already said He loves and forgives, so who are these guilty persons, and why such an extensive multi-generational punishment when grace, forgiveness and goodness abounds? Perhaps a clue is in Genesis 17:16, *for the sins of the Amorites have not yet reached their full measure.* Some nations sin from generation to generation, there's no let-up of the misery they instil, until God in His sovereignty 'breaks in' declaring the party over – Daniel 5:25-31, Babylon falls, and the Persians rise to power. These words in Exodus 34 need to be seen in terms of the comfort and reassurances they bring; God is righteous and will bring deliverance. To see them only within our culture of individualism can be misleading. Sometimes our twenty-first century lens doesn't always aid our Bible exegesis. Just as the sixteenth century Reformers were more focussed on dismantling medieval Catholicism, than genuinely trying to hear the original voices of Jesus and Paul from the New Testament texts.

in understanding God. First, it is a prayer. It's not simply a doctrinal statement; Paul words this sentence as a closing prayer for the troubled church in Corinth, using the opening word, *May*. It's a request for God's intervention on at least six levels, if not nine. Amazing how much of a petitioning prayer you can squeeze into one sentence.

Trinitarian

Though the word Father isn't used, Paul's construct here more than implies that the second statement concerning, *the love of God*, is in reference to the Father, thus connecting the prior and subsequent phrases about Jesus and the Holy Spirit.

The same happens in the most famous verse in the Bible (John 3:16), *for God so loved the world He sent His one and only Son.* The reference to Son casts the initial reference to God as the Father. That same love is referenced again in 1 John 3, explicitly linked to the Father,

> See what great love the Father has lavished on us, that we should be called children of God!
> **1 John 3:1a**

In 2 Corinthians 13:14, not only do we have reference to the Trinity, but we also have a powerful threefold title given for Jesus.

SCHOOL OF DISCIPLESHIP

Lord Jesus Christ, is a succinct and comprehensive acknowledgment of Jesus of Nazareth, being both divine and the promised Messiah.

- **Lord**, the Old Testament term used to designate God, avoiding using Yahweh, which was deemed a name too holy to even write down.

- **Jesus**, is both His human name and a description of His destiny, meaning, *saviour*.

- **Christ**, is the Greek version of the Hebrew word, Messiah, meaning the Anointed One.

Without writing an extensive essay on this, in brief, in the title, Lord Jesus Christ, we have Jesus referenced as divine, human and the long-awaited Messiah.

So, there we have a possible six-point sermon,

1. Son
    a. Lord
    b. Jesus
    c. Christ
2. Father
3. Holy Spirit

Now let's move to the next three points, that will give us a foundation for a spiritual map designed for our discipleship. Read the verse again, note that each person of the Trinity is assigned a particular attribute,

- Jesus – grace
- Father – love
- Spirit – fellowship

First, we'll define these three attributes, and then see how they work together for our discipleship.

Grace

Grace is often described as an underserved gift, receiving that which you don't deserve, whereas mercy, is not getting what you do deserve. When we think of grace in the context of Christianity, often we link it to our salvation,

> For it is by grace you have been saved, through faith – and this is not from yourselves, it is the gift of God – [9] not by works, so that no one can boast.
> **Ephesians 2:8-9**

Grace is amazing! Therefore, we mustn't limit it to the role of our salvation. Grace is an eternal attribute of God. Like love, grace is a quality of God, forever expressed in His behaviour. We see God's grace in operation in the opening chapters of the Bible. As we saw in the last chapter, God's expulsion of Adam and Eve from the garden can be seen as an act of grace rather than just a punishment. Now that sin had entered the world, the last thing our fallen nature needed was access to a tree that gave us immortality. Also, prior to the expulsion, God re-clothed their nakedness, an improved wardrobe which involved the cost of blood[52], another expression of His grace. Later, God would give His people the law, *an eye for an* eye[53], yet in Genesis 4, God chose not to kill Cain for murdering his brother – that's grace. On reading the narrative, it's as if God makes Cain a kind of travelling evangelist[54], perhaps a witness of God's grace. Sadly, problems start again when Cain stops wandering, and chooses to settle down and establish a city.

In the Gospel narrative concerning the woman caught in adultery, according to the Law, the crowd is in the right to stone her[55]. Yet, Jesus, in wisdom, dispels the crowd, and then exercises grace. Simon Peter's moving restoration on the beach by Jesus, after he had clearly denied knowing Him – grace again[56]. Peter's sin is all

---

[52] Genesis 3:21, the first blood sacrifice in the Bible, which is initiated by (a broken-hearted) God for the benefit of His humans. A sign, that the innocent will suffer in order to redeem humanity.
[53] Leviticus 24:19-20, this 'like for like' justice sought to curb the tendency for escalating actions of revenge.
[54] Genesis 4:13-17, though Cain feared retribution, God marked him so others would not kill him for his murder. The initial intention was for him to be a wander, but he gained a wife and started to build a city – I wonder what sort of people were attracted to live in the city Cain built?
[55] John 8:5
[56] John 21:15ff

the worse as he had proudly declared that he wouldn't mess up[57]; and therefore Christ's grace all the more powerful, as Peter is restored to the fold, not under a season of discipline, but as one of the Twelve, and a key church leader. I like the fact that in our Bibles, you only need to turn a single page (from John to Acts) to see Peter, restored and then freshly Spirit-filled, addressing a vast and very responsive crowd - that's grace!

The entire title Lord Jesus Christ oozes grace. That God, fully God, the **Lord** God Almighty would lower Himself and take on frail flesh, born **Jesus** in Bethlehem, and would then in obedience to His Father be anointed [**Christ**] to suffer unto death in order to rescue a fallen and corrupt world.

Therefore, grace is not simply our doctrinal currency for salvation, it is an eternal quality residing in the motivations and actions of God.

Love

This word in relation to God has surfaced in both our previous chapters. I'm also aware that some Christians struggle with the concept of God's love, or more precisely, are concerned about an over emphasis of the subject. A criticism that I've fallen foul of on more than one occasion. Such people would prefer to describe God, in terms of His absolute sovereignty and untarnished holiness, in order to set the Almighty far above our limited and

---

[57] Luke 22:33-34

corrupt concepts of human characteristics and personalities. Weirdly, or ironically? The New Testament writers often use the word holy to describe us – the believers[58].

In addition, these conservative believers would want any language of God's love to be partnered with His wrath to bring a balance to His character. In this troubled thinking two potential heresies emerge. First, such people seem to have allowed love to be redefined by *Hollywood* and pop culture, resulting in a misconception that a loving God will be soft on sin. A contemporary theologian, well published and with an internet presence, once wrote, "If you start with a God of love, you'll never end up at Calvary." The misunderstanding being, that the horrors of the Cross would be irreconcilable with an all-loving God. Obviously, they're wrong! John 3:16, explains simply and explicitly, the motivation for Calvary (Christ's sacrifice) *was* God so loving the world.

The second borderline heresy is to see God's wrath as opposite to His love. This creates a type of dualism more akin to the *ying & yang* of Eastern mysticism[59]. The misleading concept here is that

---

[58] Four examples among others, 1 Peter 2:9, Romans 1:7, Ephesians 1:1, Jude 1:3.

[59] Cosmological dualism is rife in most world beliefs and even within mainstream Christianity. It's hard to avoid, especially when the Bible talks of good and evil, spiritual warfare, and often contrasts darkness and light. Nevertheless, the wonder of the incarnation is not so much about highlighting two-sides, but the extraordinary event of the One God entering our fallen world. No longer are we operating in an 'us and them' paradigm, but as 'living sacrifices' and 'new creations' we're called to bring hope and fullness of life into the here and now. Admittedly, it's not easy to maintain

for every positive there's a negative, dark and light, good and bad, and they (unknowingly) project this thinking onto Yahweh. In the light of this, we run the risk of reducing God to a disappointed and constantly annoyed father figure, by seeing wrath as some form of justifiable vengeful anger, which we call, 'righteous anger' – thus maintaining God's holiness. This thinking can lead Christians to interpret every global disaster or atrocity as an expression of God's wrath.

The word wrath is more accurately understood as a response to injustice. To talk of extreme anger is misleading, as wrath is far more calculated and restrained. The justifiable emotion of wrath may well be felt within a person, but anger, verbal anger, lashing out, is never condoned by the Bible writers[60].

> Refrain from anger and turn from wrath;
>   do not fret – it leads only to evil.
> **Psalm 37:8**

---

such a theological ideology, when most of life is constantly divided into right and wrong, good and bad – going all the way back to the forbidden fruit of good and evil. At the end of days, God in His wisdom will separate the goats and the sheep (Matthew 25:31ff), but until then the catch in the net (to mix metaphors and Christ's parables – Matthew 13:47-49) remains unsorted – that's grace. For just as the River of God (Ezekiel 47:9) can turn saltwater fresh, who knows what Kingdom miracles can occur before the catch is eventually brought to shore?

[60] Jesus did up end the tables in the Temple. I'm not sure we can use this single proof-text to justify our own outbursts! The context is theological. The one place in the Temple's design which allowed Gentiles to be present, had been turned into a money-spinning market for the Jews. God's heart for inclusion and accessibility had been rubbished. God's wrath in His Temple swept away the injustice. It's pretty unique and particular.

SCHOOL OF DISCIPLESHIP

The Lord's Prayer holds the concepts of forgiveness and the need to avoid the temptation to do evil in proximity, as if they were related. If we understand wrath as a seething anger (or serious displeasure) in the light of witnessing injustices, then its presence shows our ability to empathise, but it mustn't surface in flawed anger, lashing out with piercing words or even violence. God's wrath is present only because of His love and holiness, and it's His enduring love and holiness that shape His wrathful responses. The Bible makes it clear, God is *slow* to anger[61], for in His wisdom and love, wrath is tempered and often expressed in outrageous acts of grace. There will be a day of vengeance, but contrast that with an entire year of His favour[62]. Wherever possible and whenever possible evil is to be overcome by good[63].

In addition, often genuine biblical wrath is only felt by the most compassionate of individuals, because it's *not* rooted in anger or revenge, but *love*. If we see wrath as separate or different to love, then we're misunderstanding it, and almost creating God in our own fallen image. Plenty of people have grown up with an annoyed and disappointed parent. Plenty of people long for a day of vengeance. It's our human nature (fallen and corrupted) that longs for these things. I believe God stands above these flawed feelings and models self-control within His greater purposes of forgiveness and restoration. We can only truly experience the

---

[61] Exodus 34:6, Nehemiah 9:17, & Jonah 4:2. The 'clearing of the Temple' is after decades of regular visits, and as God, centuries of observing the blasphemy.
[62] Isaiah 61:2
[63] Romans 12:21

genuine pain of wrath, when we see one another acting unjustly. Only then, when we witness the utter lack of love others have for each other, do such actions pull on our hearts of mercy with a seething jealousy to act and make amends. Therefore, because God so loved the world, He – painfully, costly and sacrificially – sorted it! His wrath fell on Jesus[64], in order for His love to be lavished upon us[65]. And don't forget, Jesus endured the Cross, for the joy set before Him[66], and that joy is us, our presence in eternity, our Eden-friendship restored. This wonderful salvation, these extraordinary actions, the cost, the pain, the sacrifice, were the result of God's enduring and unfailing love.

When John writes, God is love[67], he nailed it – no pun intended, even so, biblical love must be understood as gracious and strong; caring enough to confront, and willing to be the sacrificial solution to bring lasting resolution. In modern terms, you'd probably learn more about love watching a war movie than a romantic comedy.

God's love is faithful when we're faithless[68], consistent within our inconsistency. This sort of love is radical and hard for the world to fully grasp. The Gospels show that God's saving solution for humanity, was a direct threat to Roman imperialism and the Temple's religiosity. Of course, the God who knows our minds and

---

[64] 2 Corinthians 5:21
[65] 1 John 3:1
[66] Hebrews 12:2
[67] 1 John 4:8 & 16
[68] 2 Timothy 2:13

hearts, knew all this. When Christ's body was being rejected, God was showing His unfailing acceptance of us. When His body was being torn apart, God was reconciling all things together. While they threw dice to win his belongings[69], God wasn't taking any risks in winning the world. And when the most law-abiding Jew was preparing for the *annual* Passover meal, the perfect Passover Lamb[70] was being sacrificed *once and for all*[71]. At the very moment the ancient world's laws of judgment and punishment were being exercised, God chose to manifest love, mercy and grace.

The world still defaults to judgment and punishment. As a parent you may operate in this paradigm. It's hard not to. Sadly, as churches, we do the same. Our very salvation, identity and acceptance is rooted in God's love, grace and mercy. Nevertheless, when faced with someone's sin and moral failure, do we have the wisdom and love, to operate in grace and mercy, offering forgiveness and restoration? Big themes, but sadly, not for now within the limits of this book.

Fellowship

The attribute of God assigned to the Holy Spirit, in 2 Corinthians 13:14, is fellowship. Traditionally, many believers interpret this word to imply church fellowship. Thus, creating the idea that the Holy Spirit is present in our church gatherings. Let's not forget, this single verse is actually a prayer. So, if the traditional

---

[69] John 19:23
[70] John 1:29
[71] Hebrews 9:12

interpretation was true, it's still only a hope not an absolute. Though Jesus promised His presence when we gather 'in His name'[72], to activate that promise, the phrase, 'in His name' may require some deliberate actions or words, and not just the fact it's 11 o'clock on a Sunday Morning – other Sunday start times are also available.

The Greek word for fellowship, *koinonia*, carries a sense of not only meeting, but specifically meeting needs, having a shared agenda, a place of mutual edification. All helpful terms in assessing our own experience of church fellowship.

Yet, to maintain the integrity of this verse and Paul's prayer, the apostle is not thinking about a church meeting. He's talking directly and explicitly about how the Triune God encounters us in salvation. He's already highlighted grace and love, and now he concludes with the quite extraordinary privilege of fellowship. If we want to stretch the church fellowship picture, we need to remember that we ourselves are now temples of the Holy Spirit[73]. The Temple was originally built as a permanent structure to replace the Tabernacle, often called the Tent of Meeting. So, we are now that spiritual place of divine meeting, where the residing Holy Spirit within us allows true and uncluttered fellowship with God. Like Adam, back in Genesis, hearing God walking in the garden, an aspect of Eden has been restored to us.

---

[72] Matthew 18:20, note the context is Jesus talking about spiritual warfare as opposed to regular meeting.
[73] 1 Corinthians 6:19

A journey of discipleship

You may have already mapped this out for yourself. But here goes to make the chapter complete.

From 2 Corinthians 13:14, we have a pragmatic ordering of the Trinity, beginning with the work of Christ that gives us gracious access to the entire Godhead. It's by grace! In case we ever forget. So, any thoughts of unworthiness or disqualification can be disregarded, salvation is not linked to your abilities or social standing – it's grace. We all start at the same place, with an extraordinary divine gift none of us deserve.

Then, as we unwrap such an amazing gift it *should* lead us to encounter the *love* of our Heavenly Father. I've known quite mature believers take years to reach this logical step. Why so long? There's a number of reasons,

- 'Saved by grace' is more of a doctrinal statement than a relational reality that invites us to fellowship with the living God. Hence the distance and often disdain to talk of God in 'human' terms.

- Linked to the previous statement, salvation (subtly and often unknowingly) focuses on us and our sin, with God's grace being the rescue plan. Instead of a relational focus, where God's grace is the means by which we are restored and reconciled to *Abba* Father. Note, the often-quoted language of Jesus from John 14:6,

> I am the way and the truth and the life, no one comes to the father except by me.

This is not only a statement of exclusivity around the work of Jesus, but the means by which we can once again encounter the Father. Christ's death is not just about removing sin, it's about restoring relationship.

- Many people simply diminish the truth that God loves them, by concluding that He loves everyone – therefore it's neither specific nor personal, it's just a theological truth. Sometimes, behind this thinking is the unhelpful idea that you're not truly loved or even loveable. For many believers the issue of sin is still in poll position, and God's unresolved wrath is always just a divine breath away. For others the issue is linked to emotional damage. Perhaps you have low self-esteem, trust issues linked to past hurts, and the list goes on.

- For other believers, their response to God's love and grace can't simply be humble acceptance and gratitude, they create a noble work ethic, which means they're trying to be deserving of His grace. Again, this will be subtle, but nevertheless, many Christians keep themselves busy doing

God related stuff, often criticising those who seem lazy or less committed.

God doesn't love us because He has to, but because He wants to. He created us in His image, we're family, and blood is thicker than water, and the blood of Jesus – thicker still. Amen.

To recap, 2 Corinthians 13:14, God's *grace*, shockingly expressed through Christ's sacrifice, leads us to discover and encounter the true extent of God's enduring and genuine *love* for us, which invites us to partake in the extraordinary *fellowship*/friendship that is now available to us through the residing Holy Spirit. Amen.

GRACE LOVE AND FELLOWSHIP

Galatians 5:25

Since we live by the Spirit, let us keep in step with the Spirit.

CHAPTER 3

Keep in Step

LEARNING OUTCOME | To prioritise the ministry of the Holy Spirit in our sanctification and equipping, in order to avoid the frustrations of self-motivated schemes of personal improvement.

Just like a regular school, let's do a quick recap. Last time we examined Paul's prayer of 2 Corinthians 13:14. In church circles this verse is called 'The Grace', and it's often recited from memory by a congregation straining their necks as they attempt to speak the words over each other whilst gaining some fleeting eye-contact. Without doubt, it is a great prayer, calling one another into the knowledge of Christ's grace, God's love and to fellowship with the Holy Spirit. Yet it does lead to an obvious question,

How do we fellowship with the Holy Spirit?

SCHOOL OF DISCIPLESHIP

To learn of God's grace we can read the first half of the book of Romans and Ephesians chapter 2. To grasp the concept of God's love, reading 1 John would be a good place to start. However, what am I to read to deepen my friendship with God's Spirit? Well, we could do a word study and follow the paperchase across the two Testaments to find proof-texts of the Spirit's ministry and character. But before we thumb through the entire Bible, underlining relevant and less relevant verses, let's start with a single stand-alone verse that both captures the heart of discipleship, and a foundational approach to all Christian ministry,

> Since we live by the Spirit, let us keep in step with the Spirit.
> **Galatians 5:25**[74]

It's as simple as that. However, as a wise Argentinian pastor once pointed out to me, *simple* isn't always *easy*. Remind me, what's the greatest commandment? Oh yeah, love God with the whole of your being and love everyone else. Simple. Simple to remember, simple to state in one sentence. Easy to do? Well, that's an entirely different matter.

Let's put Galatians 5:25 into context. Hopefully, we'll discover some familiar language, and also detect the temptation to move away from simple, in order to embrace something, we may mistakenly think is easier.

---

[74] *Keep in step* = other English translations have *walk, follow*, even, *surrender to* (Aramaic Bible in Plain English). The actual Greek word is, *stoichōmen* – to walk in step with.

KEEP IN STEP

Does the following ring any bells?

> But the fruit of the Spirit is love, joy, peace, forbearance, kindness, goodness, faithfulness, [23] gentleness and self-control. Against such things there is no law.
> **Galatians 5:22-23**

Now, I need to fess up, before I criticise others, as I'm just as guilty in the way I've traditionally handled these verses. Perhaps even more so, than many of you, as a preacher and Bible teacher for over 30 years. Many of us have memorised these verses, we know the nine fruit of the Spirit off by heart. We've drawn pictures for our children's work. We've even used different fruit to illustrate the nine attributes named in the verses. Or, in staying truer to the original text, we've used the example of an orange – one fruit but split into nine separate segments. You can never accuse the church of lacking imagination and creativity. In my past I even helped compose a child-friendly song based on the nine fruit.

So, we have our illustrations, different fruits or citrus segments, and now comes the all-important application. It's always important to have an application. Nevertheless, our best intentions (and colourful picture) only serve to form an endless and unachievable piece of homework, as we challenge each other to have these nine attributes of God manifesting daily in our lives.

SCHOOL OF DISCIPLESHIP

Our application of these verses often went something like this; meditate on all nine words. Now ask yourself, which one is missing in my life? Which one is a struggle to manifest? Is it joy, gentleness, self-control – which is it? Take your time and be honest.

To aid the process, we might add clearer definitions to each of the nine words. In order to clarify we're all on the same page as we deliberately chew over each fruit segment. By the way, what is the difference between goodness and kindness?

Pause. Are you taking notes, thinking I've written the outline and response for a future Bible study? Or are you detecting my subtle cynicism. I suspect something intended to be *simple*, has now become a far more contrived weight around our necks.

In Galatians 5:21-22, we're meant to be thinking about the fruit of the Spirit, not our weaknesses and short comings. In many ways, Paul is sharing the exact opposite of what we've perceived from the passage. Paul is celebrating the breadth of the Spirit's character, the same Spirit residing and shaping our lives. It's a releasing revelation. Whereas in the church we've written down a list of nine characteristics we pretty much feel are all out of our daily reach. For years, I felt like the Holy Spirit was setting me homework, He wanted me to develop nine specific qualities to improve my character.

KEEP IN STEP

In management theory, regarding presentational skills, there's something called the rule of three or four. Basically, people are better at remembering three or four points rather than more. Hence the traditional three-point sermon, and using an alliteration or a mnemonic, is even more helpful. I once heard someone preach on the nine fruit of the Spirit. As he introduced the subject you could feel the congregation sigh with expected exhaustion. Nine points! And yes, he did, he preached a nine-point sermon. Which to be honest, I can't remember any of the content, apart from the use of an orange to aid his points. I *know* what his nine points were, I *knew* his points before he preached them. To be honest I just remember thinking this sermon will go down as an example of how not to structure a sermon. And hey, I was right.

The nine fruit are not presented as homework, they convey the character of the Holy Spirit, and by Trinitarian unity, the character of God. They're not a complete list. The most noticeable absence being – grace. When Paul in Romans writes down the fruit of the Kingdom, his list is a perfect three, righteousness, peace and joy[75] – memorable. Though note the additional attribute of righteousness, which isn't found in his earlier[76] Galatians list, thus proving these nine fruit are part of a flowing description of God, as opposed to an absolute prescribed definition of a 'good' Christian.

---

[75] Romans 14:17
[76] Earlier, chronologically, though in the final canon of Scripture, Romans comes before Galatians in the New Testament.

SCHOOL OF DISCIPLESHIP

Meet the Holy Spirit

Welcome to the Holy Spirit, the residing presence of God making our frail bodies a temple[77] – a holy and sacred space. The Spirit exudes, love, joy, peace, patience, kindness, goodness, faithfulness, gentleness and self-control[78]. Now, this amazing person, of the Holy Spirit has chosen to dwell within us. Therefore, it's not our homework to acquire these Godly characteristics, it's our job to surrender to His residing presence, by crucifying our natural tendencies[79] and allowing His ministry to work within us, and to shine out from us. In brief, for us to truly live by the Spirit, we need to keep in step with the Spirit.

So, Galatians 5:25 gets it in a nutshell. But (historically) we've decided to unpack, (dissect, pictorially represent, and sing) verses

---

[77] 1 Corinthians 6:19

[78] Does God need self-control? No, He already has it, as stated by Paul in this verse! But why self-control? For mercy to triumph over judgment (James 2:13), for grace to curb His wrath (John 8:10-11) and for the kindness of God to lead us to repentance (Romans 2:4).

[79] Galatians 5:24, the verse that nestles between the fruit (v22-23) and the instruction (v25) requires far more than a footnote. Crucifying our natural tendencies and desires can be a life's work – which is real frustration I am trying to avoid! Romans 6 highlights this issue, with the infuriating struggle that follows outlined in Romans 7. Some Christians believe Romans 7 (*For what I want to do I do not do, but what I hate I do* v15b) is a prescription not a description of the Christian's struggle. They resign themselves to the reality of failure. Whereas Paul is building to Romans 8, often sub-headed *Life in the Spirit*. Which brings us back to Galatians 5, Paul's earlier writing, which starts with a call to freedom, the dangers of becoming religious, the stark contrast between the 'world' and 'spirit' living and the need to change by being attached to the Spirit. Then, in case we missed the point, Galatians 6:1 says it all over again, as both a pastoral instruction and a warning. It's *simple*, but not *easy*. However, where we place the emphasis will shape (or misshape) our spiritual lives.

KEEP IN STEP

22 & 23 with the additional help of online dictionaries to lay down a challenge few of us can ever accomplish.

We've attempted to take the simple (though not easy) and turn it into something far more convoluted, yet weirdly, far more accessible in application with the help of a dictionary and an orange!

At a week-long youth event some years ago, the subject matter for one of the evening talks was the 'Gifts of the Spirit'[80]. The appointed leader for that evening's teaching chose to move the goal posts and spoke instead on the fruit of the Spirit, with nine definitions and a final challenge to the teenage audience to all try harder.

On reflection, another leader present told me[81],

> *"Why do we do this? Why change the subject from gifts to fruit? We could have had a response time with people prophesying, praying for healings and speaking in tongues. The response would have been immediate and tangible. After all they're gifts, graciously given, instantly received, and ready for use. How on earth will we know if anyone has*

---

[80] Traditionally recognised as those listed in 1 Corinthians 12:7-10, Romans 12:6-8, and Ephesians 4:11.
[81] What follows is a paraphrase, I didn't record the conversation or memorise the actual words.

become more patient or kind? Fruit, by definition, takes time to mature."

They were right. You can't just swap gifts for fruit and ignore the metaphor in the process.

The differences are important. Gifts, like most gifts can be easily received, unwrapped and enjoyed. Fruit requires time. Perhaps that's one of the points of Paul's inspired illustration. It will take time but not because we need to cultivate these nine specific attributes, but because we need to learn, how to keep in step with the Spirit; nurture a life of being filled, re-filled and guided. If *fellowship* with the Holy Spirit is similar (linguistically) to *friendship* with the Holy Spirit, then we're back in the realms of relationship building, back in Eden and those *daily* encounters with God.

The sacrifice of the Cross and the triumph of the Empty Tomb allows us access to God, but not so He can give us homework! The victory of these events restores a broken relationship. By grace, we can discover first-hand the love of God and have the privilege of fellowshipping with the Holy Spirit – Please, never forget the significance of 2 Corinthians 13:14? The challenge of fellowshipping with the Spirit, is not primarily about being patient, gentle and good, but staying in step with God's lead.

This is how Jesus explained the exact same situation,

KEEP IN STEP

> Jesus gave them this answer: 'Very truly I tell you, the Son can do nothing by himself; he can do only what he sees his Father doing, because whatever the Father does the Son also does.
> **John 5:19**

Throughout His ministry, Jesus is attentive to His Father's will and workings. Perhaps that's why He woke early each morning to pray[82], to get the latest update and news about His Father's business[83]. In times of worship, I love to walk around the room. Obviously not if I'm being overwhelmed by His presence and lying on the floor. However, if I have a leadership role for that particular meeting, I love to look in the natural to discern what God is doing in the spiritual. I ask myself prayerful questions,

- What's the Spirit doing?
- Where are the angels?
- Where are the demons?

This is my spiritual reconnaissance. Also, please note, like good intelligence gathering, I don't need to go public with my findings. Rather, like the value of wartime reconnaissance, I need to allow my findings to influence my ministry decisions. If you long for genuine Spirit-led meetings, then your preparation must be able to incorporate the flexibility to respond to the needs discerned in the room. If I'm down to preach that morning, do I launch

---

[82] Mark 1:35. It was undoubtedly this discipline, regularly observed by His disciples, that led to their request, "Lord, teach us to pray." (Luke 11:1)
[83] Luke 2:49, *'my Father's house'* or, *'about my Father's business'*, always a preoccupation and priority.

thoughtlessly into my prayerfully prepared script[84], or do I react to the real-time activity of God in the room? We need to learn to do church differently, just as we need to reassess our approach to discipleship. In brief, we need to be aware of the person of the Holy Spirit, just as much (if not more) than the doctrines of the Holy Scriptures. For it is those very Scriptures that call us and challenge us to stay in step with the Spirit and take note of what the Father is doing.

Recently I read several reports about a university campus-based revival. Students were desiring to gather, to worship, pray, and be biblically inspired. Hundreds gathered daily. The various reports recorded very similar reflections.

- The simplicity of the meetings. Corporate worship, waiting on God, then a practical Bible message, with clear application and plenty of space to respond.
- The simplicity of the worshipping musicians. A minimalistic band set-up, sometimes just two people. The use of accessible and repeatable songs.
- The simple relevance of the Bible teaching. Deliberately within the university context, being more motivational and challenging, than informative and instructive.
- Space. Whether in actual quiet or using simple songs, there was time given for people to reflect, spiritually 'push-

---

[84] The use of *thoughtlessly* and *prayerfully* are deliberate to show that no matter our prior preparation, God's actual *living* presence must be honoured!

in', respond, open their hearts to God, and receive prayer from others.
- Time. It was said to be hard to fully identify when one scheduled meeting ended, and another began. Time became irrelevant.

Obviously as people visited and talked about what was going on, the inevitable question was raised. "Can we have this in our church?"

And the honest answer is, "No."

Here's a reminder of those common and repeated comments.

- unrestricted time
- simplicity and repetition in the corporate worship
- space to respond

Most Sunday services can't offer that. Though, my heart would love to see a revolution in our approach to corporate worship and especially the function of praise – please read my earlier book, **School of Praise**[85] to hear my heart on this. I'm still praying for a lasting restoration of praise to its biblical origins to sweep across our congregations. Where we can create space to encounter the living God rather than eclipsing His agenda with our inflexible song-lists and other programmed 'necessities'. Oh, to be able to

---
[85] Available on Amazon.

take a much-needed break, to step back, and deeply breathe in the inspirational Holy Spirt, and then to worship *simply* 'in Spirit and in truth'[86] – *simple*, though not necessarily *easy*. I've even witnessed on a handful of occasions, when the gathered faithful have been so 'in Spirit and in truth', that their failure to be in *tune* didn't quench God's activity. Read my book, as referenced earlier in this paragraph, to understand these things more and discover some practical and biblical solutions.

How do we keep in step with the Spirit?

Prayer – the Christian's vital breath[87]. There is no shortcut or alternative in building a Holy Spirit relationship than through the essential discipline of prayer. However, that prayer can also be in the shape of a corporate gathering of like-minded spiritually hungry believers who find the time to get lost in wonder,

> These were priceless moments, where God's grace could handle our ignorance within the honesty of our zeal.

---

[86] John 4:24, this is Jesus's direct and explicit description of *corporate worship*, as the context is about sacred places. His answer, worship is a *spiritual* discipline requiring our complete *honesty*.

[87] I've stolen this phrase from a book of the same title by L. A. T Van Dooren ©1961.

love and praise[88]. I was blessed throughout my early years of spiritual formation to hang out with such spiritually hungry people. Some of them were not great theologians, so in later life I needed to modify some of my thinking, Thankfully, I discovered that genuine unintentional bad biblical exegesis doesn't always eclipse the loving and dynamic presence of God. These were priceless moments, where God's grace could handle our ignorance within the honesty of our zeal. The lesson I learnt – nothing can replace time with God, God honours those who honour Him.

To keep in step with the Spirit, re-read the Gospel narratives and observe Jesus doing what He's discerning from the Father. Learn to become less presumptuous of a meetings shape and contents. Deliberately give space to God's Spirit. We keep in step through prayer, through praise and through operating in the gifts of discernment and prophecy. My earlier book, **School of Prophecy**[89] presents a biblical foundation and model for safe prophetic practise, as well as a detailed outline to help nurture and mature the gift of prophecy in the local church.

Finally, take your time, 'keeping in step' is a relational principal, which is an important aspect of any developing friendship. Though time on your own with God is essential for discipleship, depending on your learning preferences, and the 'voices' you

---

88 A wonderful phrase from the last line of Charles Wesley's hymn, Love Divine All Love's Excelling.
89 Available on Amazon.

already might have untamed living rent free in your head[90], such times may not be that beneficial at the start of your journey. As I've already stated, learn with others. Christianity is designed for the corporate, it's a community, the local church should operate as a spiritual family. If you're part of a weekly home group (house group, small group, life group, community group, cell group) decide together to make *effective* discipleship an ongoing learning outcome and introduce the notion of fellowshipping with the Holy Spirit and learning to keep in step with the Spirit. Alternatively, or in addition, find that prayer group in your locality, that priorities praise for the sake of strategic intercession. I've regularly been blessed by stumbling across such Spirit-infused people. Sometimes this has been a church home group led by a couple hungry for the things of the Spirit. Or a para-church group with spiritual intensity that isn't being restricted by local congregational politics. Pray for divine appointments, meeting the right people with the right agenda. Such encounters at different times led me to enrol on my life-changing Christian gap year, talking in tongues, moving in prophecy, even a supposedly random conversation in central Italy, led me to explore a specific theological training college, thus launching my accredited church ministry.

---

[90] I've often said, 'Like an airport, but when we arrive in the Kingdom of God, there's no *baggage reclaim*.' Unfortunately, we often bring past traumas, flaws and bad habits with us. So, until some of these issues are resolved, our minds renewed and demonic influences expelled – time on our own can prove troublesome for a small minority.

KEEP IN STEP

Pay attention! If we take the phrase *'keep in step'* literally, then Spirit-led Christianity has momentum. If you're not growing, not being stretched, or worse, getting bored. Stop! Pray. Wait. Listen. Then carefully and wisely re-evaluate the place you find yourself in. Use others you trust in this final process too.

I love the almost chilling words of God to Elijah, *What are you doing here?*[91]

God wasn't saying *'here'*, geographically, but *'here'*, emotionally[92]. Listen to what the Spirit is saying to you right now, perhaps He's asking the same question. We often talk of being at a crossroads in our lives, when sometimes we're actually living in a cul-de-sac.

Keeping in step with the Spirit requires a mix of spiritual disciplines and *space* – space to connect with God in our everyday. Like the fruit of the Spirit in Galatians 5:21-22, it's not a definitive list, it's the daily choice to stay aware and attentive to the presence of God, thus allowing Him to form a consistent spiritual lifestyle.

I'm no dancer. My body just doesn't move to music like it ought. Other people can instantly sway to the rhythm – effortlessly. Though I did teach myself to play the guitar. One hand strums the rhythm, the other needs to find the shape of chords by placing

---

[91] 1 Kings 19:10b
[92] Elijah had just won a great victory on Mount Carmel; God was indeed God. Yet he was now running in fear of his life, perhaps logically, but not in the context of serving such a great God. Elijah in 1 Kings 19 is struggling emotionally.

different fingers at different positions on the guitar's neck. It's not easy! At first it hurts, and there is nothing at all natural about forcing your fingers to hold down thin steel strings in weird shapes. In addition, once you've mastered one chord you need to find the fingering for the next. Then to play a song, you need to change chords swifty. How did such a discipline ever come into existence? Yet, somehow it works, and eventually your fingers learn the positions and can find them without your eyes needing to see[93]. Some of us need to persevere again with God's Spirit. We've taken an alternative, perhaps an *easier* approach to Christianity, whilst neglecting the *simple* instruction to keep in step with God.

Finally, I love this verse,

> But solid food is for the mature, who because of practice have their **senses** trained to distinguish between good and evil.
> **Hebrews 5:14 [NASB]** *(my emphasis)*

A mark of maturity is discernment. Annoyingly 'discernment' has increasingly become my answer to so many ministry skills' questions.

- How do you pastor into this situation?

---

[93] For the geeks among you, in addition to our five physical senses (sight, hearing, taste, smell and touch), we have proprioception, spacial awareness, for example, close your eyes and place the tip of your index finger onto the end of your nose. Did you find it? Touch-typists, most musicians, and the majority of us when we walk use this natural inner perception.

KEEP IN STEP

- How do you lead worship in this scenario?
- How did you know to ask *that* question[94]?

Here in Hebrews, it's our senses that are being used in this spiritual development. The word *senses* isn't present in every English translation, though the word (*aisthētēria*), meaning *sensory abilities* is in the original Greek. I personally believe that all five of our natural senses can be used spiritually to discern the work the spiritual realm.

There are some clues in Scripture to this affect. Many people see visions[95], and hear God's voice[96]. We're called to taste God[97], and to detect the difference between the stench of death and the aroma of Christ[98]. Through the laying on of hands we can bring spiritual impartation and healing[99].

Prophetic symbolism is when a simple symbol is used prophetically in a way that aids healing[100] or some form of spiritual breakthrough[101]. I've been in meetings where the sound of coins hitting a hard floor has symbolised the breaking of chains – not

---

[94] Jesus's conversation with the woman of Sameria is a lesson in discernment and prophecy. John 4:7-26, as is Paul's encounter on entering Ephesus in Acts 19:1-7.
[95] Too many! Read the book of Zechariah. But especially note the unique exchange between Elisha and his servant in 2 Kings 6:16-17.
[96] Perhaps most famously the boy Samuel, 1 Samuel 3:10.
[97] Metaphorically, Psalm 34:8 & 1 Peter 2:3, and prophetically Jeremiah 15:16 & Ezekiel 3:3.
[98] 2 Corinthians 2:15-16
[99] Luke 4:40, Acts 8:17 & 1 Timothy 4:14
[100] Acts 19:11-12
[101] 2 Kings 13:18-19

SCHOOL OF DISCIPLESHIP

just a physical sound, but an actual spiritual breakthrough moment for many. On another occasion, someone had brought a household door and its frame to a meeting. We were then encouraged to walk through the door. Some were symbolically leaving the past. Others in faith, stepping into their spiritual destiny. Weird? I was one of those participants and it worked[102]! Sometimes when our faith connects with something physical it can help us engage and fully believe. Call it a gimmick or call it a proven educational aid. Jesus used the everyday in His parables and the prophet Agabus used Paul's own belt to bind him to speak into his imminent arrest[103].

The Bible consists of different literary genres, historical narratives, poetry, parables and an enormous number of prophetic actions and imagery. All contain truth. All have value and purpose. Be careful not to assume that that which is symbolic is powerless, or that which is sensory is subjective. God can infuse the physical with His presence – and that's when miracles happen[104].

---

[102] 1998 was a year of change. Different and unexpected life-changing opportunities opened up to us. We saw God miraculously accelerate processes to relocate us into new jobs, new ministries and a new home.

[103] Acts 21:10-11

[104] I'm not talking about the doctrine of transubstantiation! I was thinking about the feeding of the five thousand, the healing of leprosy, and the restoration of sight to the blind.

KEEP IN STEP

1 Thessalonians 5:23-24

May God himself, the God of peace, sanctify you through and through. May your whole spirit, soul and body be kept blameless at the coming of our Lord Jesus Christ. ²⁴The one who calls you is faithful and he will do it.

CHAPTER 4

BODY SOUL AND SPIRIT

LEARNING OUTCOMES | To gain a holistic understanding of Christian discipleship. To discover some key disciplines that will develop our wellbeing.

In 1 Thessalonians 5:23, Paul talks of us as being body, soul and spirit. Though he places them in the opposite order, prioritising the spirit, yet knowing (as a Hebrew) that these three components are intrinsically linked, and having been created in the image of God[105], we function better from the inside out. We know from modern society, that those who become overly concerned about their physical appearance generally struggle emotionally with an irrational and misplaced body image. Ordering our lives (spirit,

---

[105] Genesis 1:26

soul and body), like ordering aright our work tasks, makes us efficient, productive and far less stressed[106].

I don't want to enter theological debate of understanding the dichotomy, or the trichotomy of humankind[107]. I just want to state that in the same way we're told to take regular exercise for our physical wellbeing, we've now learnt (hopefully) that our mental health also requires attention. I would therefore suggest that we also need to monitor our spiritual health. You've probably heard of the abbreviation IQ, *intelligence quotient*, a means of quantifying a person's intelligence, that relates to their cognitive abilities. The term EQ, *emotional quotient*, also exists within the discipline of psychology. In this context, it's not about EQ *audio equalizing* and a row of technical switches on a sound desk. Our emotional quotient (or, emotional intelligence) seeks to monitor how we recognise, understand and respond skilfully to our emotions. In addition to these two heavily documented areas, we could also introduce SQ, *spiritual quotient*, a means to understanding and developing our spiritual intelligence.

---

[106] John Maxwell, *Equip Course*, suggests doing the right 20% of your work will achieve 80% of your targets, because not all tasks are equal in value and importance. Key to your work-health is the ability to accurately order and prioritise your tasks with the appropriate allocation of time.

[107] When talking of humans within a religious context, *dichotomy*, suggests we consist of a physical body and a soul; *trichotomy*, we consist of a body, soul and spirit.

BODY SOUL AND SPIRIT

In Ephesians 1:17, Paul prays for the church to receive the *Spirit of wisdom and revelation*[108]. This isn't two things, wisdom *and* revelation, but the presence of spiritual wisdom, which, by definition, requires revelation. We need divine insights into the Scriptures that God has given to us and the spiritual discernment to receive and weigh prophetic support for specific situations.

A re-reading of Ephesians will reveal a list of quite extensive truths and challenges that many of us may have glossed over.

- 1:3 *Praise be to God... who has blessed us in the heavenly realms[109] with every spiritual blessing in Christ.*
- 1:18-20 To grasp that the power working in us is the same as that which raised Christ from the dead. Echoed in 3:20
- 2:6 We are seated with Christ in the heavenly realms.
- 3:10 Our job is to make known God's wisdom to the rulers and powers in the heavenly realms.

---

[108] The word *Spirit* could be translated *spirit,* either Paul is praying for an increase of God's Holy Spirit upon the church in regard to wisdom and revelation, or for the church to receive, like a spiritual gift, greater levels of spiritual wisdom and revelation.

[109] The *spiritual realms* are only explicitly named in this epistle. Paul talks of a third heaven in 2 Corinthians 12:2, a paradise of inexpressible things. The term heaven in Hebrew (as in modern Spanish) can denote the sky as well as the more spiritual understanding of the place where God dwells. Therefore, the notion of three heavens is born. First, within the physical realm, where the heavens above, simply means the sky and the stars beyond. The third heaven as already noted refers to the celestial courts, akin to imagery in the Book of Revelation, chapters 4 & 5 particularly. The *second heaven* or *heavenly realms* is a recognition of the spiritual reality that inhabits our physical reality. Technically, it's the place where angels and demons dwell. It's where Christ is establishing His dominion, and where we (the church) are doing battle with forces hostile to God and destructive to human lives – as described by Paul throughout his letter to the Ephesians. For a humble footnote, that's quite long enough for now.

- 3:17-19 to grasp the width, length, height and depth of Christ's love, a surpassing knowledge that fills you with the fullness of God – that sounds like SQ more than IQ to me.
- 5:18-20 to be filled with the Holy Spirit, that in these verses brings song and thanksgiving, as opposed to wisdom and revelation in 1:17.
- 6:10-18 Spiritual warfare, spiritual equipping and spiritual strategy.

Getting a hold of these extraordinary biblical truths, along with getting our heads around the reality of heavenly realm activity and our part within it, all speaks to our SQ levels.

When we get our *made-in-the-image-of-God* ordering correct, then it will be our heightened SQ levels that will start to affect and strengthen our EQ levels, and even our general physical wellbeing – who knows, our IQ might increase too.

Body Soul and Spirit

The body is our physical form, that will one day cease to be. Our spirit is that which connects us to God, who Himself is spirit[110]. Even in our fallen nature, the reality of a spirit can be detected in people's longing for something to worship, for a sense of meaning, or a purpose. I believe we're designed to worship God, and so if we're not, we will most probably worship something else.

---

[110] John 3:5-7 & 4:24

Hence the plethora of fan clubs, devout followers and groupies, not forgetting the more recent trend for taking selfies. Plenty of people still love to worship themselves.

Finally, the soul is a helpful designation for our inner self.

- our mind – what we're thinking
- our emotions – how we're feeling
- our will – the decisions we're making

Ancient Greek thought loved to compartmentalise life. So, their dichotomy and trichotomy theories of humanity sought to dissect and separate how humans functioned. Hebraic thought (as seen in the Bible) was far more holistic. Though the categories of body, soul and spirit can be referenced to aid understanding, they can't actually be separated in reality, all three exist, overlap, and interlock, and affect each other. So that, when we suffer from a 24-hour cold, we can still feel rough, demotivated, and find it hard to concentrate. It's a physical affliction with emotional consequences. And if we really can't be bothered to read our Bible, because we're running a high temperature – don't panic, we're not spiritually back-sliding! We've just got a cold, that's all.

As mentioned, our soul is often described with three aspects, thoughts, feelings and decisions. For example, happy thoughts, make for happy feelings, which often lead to making healthy decisions. Alternatively, a specific bad memory, may conjure up feelings of anger, which could then lead to a highly destructive decision.

Now throw these things together with your body and spirit. A happy person will most probably be stress free and motivated to do something healthy rather than destructive. If they're a believer, when happy, they're often more aware of God's presence, leading to a desire to be thankful, to praise God, resulting in better levels of discernment, leading to better, and often less selfish decisions.

It's not strictly formulaic, or necessarily a reliable linear progression. However, often a simple physical walk in the countryside may clear your head, calm your thoughts and help you engage with God through the beauty of His creation. Hence the reason for the holistic Hebraic mindset, these things can't be pulled apart and compartmentalised. Life happens on all fronts, all the time. When we neglect an area, we neglect our entire wellbeing.

Now that we've started to embrace an understanding of the holistic nature of our being, this can raise vital questions about our discipleship. Are we growing, body, soul and spirit? Or, like our Greco-Romans forefathers, are we choosing to compartmentalise our lives. We cultivate acceptable behaviour for a Sunday gathering, but act and *sound* very different when we're cheering on our football team later that same day. How much screen time do we willingly give to our mobiles, compared to the time we give communing with God? I'm not saying they need to be the same, or that spiritual things need to be more, that thinking leads to religion. I'm more interested in our emotions, how motivated are we in attending a midweek Bible study, and how do those feelings compare to chilling out in front of the television?

Let's not get legalistic or religious about these things. Here's some questions for you.

- Do romantic stories or self-pity sulks get all your tears?
- When did you last weep in a time of worship?
- When did you weep for the spiritually lost, the emotionally broken-hearted, or those needing supernatural grace to be sustained through prolonged seasons of pain or oppression?

When I first encountered laughter as a manifestation of the Spirit of God, it was healing, releasing, and refreshing. I love God-instigated laughter in times of corporate worship. I don't want all my laughter to be given to stand-up comics, or some slapstick family movie. For me, tears and laughter form part of my sacrifice of praise. Worship songs have the potential to minister to my body, soul and spirit. This can also be reflected in my need to stand, or kneel, or raise my hands, the volume of my voice, the expression on my face, and the joy in my posture[111]. In times of

---

[111] Interestingly, there are specific Hebrew words, often simply translated *praise* in our English translations, that describe some of these physical actions. It's as if God knew that these responses were going to be distinct manifestations of praise beyond singing songs. Find out more in my publication, **School of Praise**.

corporate praise, I seek to give opportunity for the Spirit's fresh conviction, or for a new expression of His presence to be voiced as a prophetic utterance. I do this by allowing my spiritual thoughts to connect to the songs, discovering their Scriptural links and letting my mind find other Bible truths to resonate with my spirit. Sounds complicated? Well, what do you do when singing songs for 10 or 15 minutes? These songs are rarely great works of art requiring our full attention to the subtle nuisances in the music. Deliberately, they're short and simple in musical composition. Written for congregational use and (hopefully) to give space to our minds to interact with their presenting truths. Find out more in my earlier publication, **School of Praise**. Rather than rubbing along with the disenchanted cynics, who find our modern worship songs seriously lacking in quality, start to embrace why these songs, as opposed to hymns from a previous era, are deliberately simple. Then the challenging reality of genuine biblical praise, 'in spirit and in truth' will hit us in very familiar language – *simple*, but not necessarily *easy*. To engage in genuine Spirit-led and heart-responding praise requires sacrifice[112]. Though it may be much easier (and feel more substantial) to sing some classic hymn accompanied with good instrumentation, than to lay your body, soul and spirit bare before the presence of God.

Never forget, our body, soul and spirit are linked. God's redemption and restoration comes with benefits. Over the years, I've witnessed those benefits and blessings manifest emotionally,

---

[112] Hebrews 13:15

spiritually and physically upon people. For a time, I was a widower. Then God graciously and wonderfully placed an amazing woman in my path. One day we had lunch together in her city, and I needed to rush back to my hometown to offer a lift to some friends for an evening prayer meeting. I was running a little late, as I entered my friends' house, one of them took one look at me and exclaimed, "Wow! You've obviously had a good day, what's her name?"

My countenance had changed. My face, unbeknown to me, was freely displaying something of the new joy in my life[113]. I've witnessed this time and again among new believers. As people leave behind destructive life choices, finding inexpressible joy replacing anxiety, and peace replacing once unsurmountable levels of stress. Healthier emotions become reflected in our physical being; emotions that are shaped by the presence of spiritual truths. Our humanity consists of three components, each has its value, and they are inseparable from the other two. Sadly, when they are forced apart, all sorts of issues can occur. Unrealistic expectations and an unhealthy behaviour around our physical wellbeing. A plethora of mental issues. Even extreme and destructive religious beliefs and practices. We live in a world, where our bodies, souls and spirits can be preyed upon by unrealistic expectations and misinformation through exploiting our weaknesses. Gyms, plastic surgery, and even some therapists

---

[113] I'm suddenly reminded of Moses, and the fact that his face would start to shine when he had spent time in God's presence. Exodus 34:30 & 2 Corinthians 3:7

are making good business out of our vulnerability. Sadly, so too are religious cults and manipulative churches.

Business is business, and our insecurities are constantly being targeted, like a computer virus endlessly trying to penetrate our firewall to steal our identity. Never has our personal identity been such a prominent battleground. New Testament salvation offers us redemption, forgiveness, restoration, access to God, and His residing presence within us. Plus, the strengthening language of adoption, a new citizenship, being a new creation and our new identity of being in Christ[114]. We've got it all *and some*! Yet the prince of the air, that liar from the beginning[115], has riddled our society with their plague of deceptions and counterfeit alternatives. Even Christians are not immune to occasionally falling foul to this vile distorted creature that manifests so convincingly as a messenger of light[116].

Effective discipleship will always require feeding from God's words, daily prayer and regular fellowship. However, the importance of why we need these disciplines needs to be made clear. I'm sure in an alternative book about discipleship you'll find a chapter on the Bible, one on prayer and another on attending church. Later in this publication we will address these things directly; but first we need to understand the context and value of

---

[114] Romans 8:15, Ephesians 2:19, 2 Corinthains 5:17 and Galatians 3:27
[115] Ephesians 2:2, John 8:44
[116] 2 Corinthians 11:14

these God resources in ministering to our whole being – body, soul and spirit.

Mindfulness and physical wellbeing

Regarding mindfulness, you can probably find the same list of things to do on any social media site. Whether it's being presented by a qualified psychologist or a self-declared life-coach, their *to do* list will generally look the same.

1. Get more sleep
2. Do some form of daily physical exercise
3. Engage in a healthy diet
4. Be exposed to natural sunlight
5. Incorporate a twice-weekly period of meditation, or take timeout to appreciate the natural world
6. And finally, choose to hang around supportive and encouraging people.

There's your starter for six, to instantly improve your wellbeing. Make number 5 your devotional life with God, and number 6 attending a good church – and you're sorted.

Sometimes Christian discipleship is rooted in common sense. You don't need a personal prophecy to tell you that quality sleep, a healthy diet and regular physical exercise are good for you. And not only for your body, but remember, they all feed positively into your mental and spiritual health too.

Let's now look again at the six-point list, but this time through our spiritual eyes.

1. Sleep

In Mark we find Jesus in a boat, sleeping whilst a life-threatening storm raged around Him[117]. This is a remarkable example of calmly handling a situation that for everyone else was massively stressful. People normally lose sleep due to overactive minds, often linked to worries and anxiety. If I really wanted to prove the importance of sleep, I'd be better off asking a medic to write this paragraph, than clutching at a single Bible passage that mentions sleep. But I conclude spiritually, any storm you can sleep through you'll undoubtedly have authority over – just like Jesus.

Here's another example, that really *crosses-the-line* regarding over spiritualising a Bible narrative. Adam's answer to his loneliness was created by God while he was asleep![118] Yeah, yeah... I know it's stretch, I'm just saying, it's *there* in the Bible. Perhaps in our *resting*, God gets the space to recalibrate our problems and worries. How often have you heard people say 'sleep on it' or 'it will seem better in the morning'. Sleep works wonders.

---

[117] Mark 4:37-38
[118] Genesis 2:21

BODY SOUL AND SPIRIT

My journey with Jesus began when I was thirteen. I knew little to nothing about true Christianity and had no church experience. Yet one night, Jesus met me in a dream. When I woke, I knew – I wanted to know more. It was Friday morning, on Sunday afternoon with the aid of an evangelistic tract, I gave my life to Jesus. Sleep is great and spiritual dreams are a bonus!

> In peace I will lie down and sleep, for you alone, Lord, make me dwell in safety.
> **Psalm 4:8**

> It is futile for you to rise up early,
> To stay up late,
> To eat the bread of painful labour;
> For he grants sleep to his beloved sleep
> **Psalm 127:2**

> There remains, then, a Sabbath-rest for the people of God; [10] for anyone who enters God's rest also rests from their works, just as God did from his. [11] Let us, therefore, make every effort to enter that rest, so that no one will perish by following their example of disobedience.
> **Hebrews 4:9-11**

God's promised Sabbath-rest is an entire topic of its own. So very briefly, sleep is God's design for our physical and mental rest and rejuvenation. The Sabbath-rest is God's assurance that if we take timeout (responsibly) He has it covered – it's a day of trust, not to strive, but believing that all will be well even in the absence of our constant efforts. This was a regular mandatory requirement for

God's people – to keep the sabbath[119]. 'In Christ', I believe this physical 24-hour period, becomes a spiritual and mental lifestyle practice – trusting God in everything. Nevertheless, it remains a challenge to find significant space to rest and trust God for the everyday.

Modern society is robbing us of sleep. Not only linked to worries, but often through a poor work-life balance (there's just not enough hours in the day!), plus (for some) excessive screen-time on our chosen device, especially last thing at night, all these things will deprive us of good sleep. At many residential conferences that I've been a speaker at, I have felt led to pray for people's improved sleep patterns. It's not really prophecy, to ask if there are people present struggling with sleep, it's a sad reality and a byproduct of our present environment.

Sleep! Get it, even if you need a miracle through prayer to still your troubled mind or improve your breathing patterns when asleep.

2. Activity
Our bodies need frequent physical exercise – it's a fact, deal with it. Also, our minds need to be stimulated, my parents did crossword puzzles, and even won national competitions. I use an app on my phone to keep my brain active through doing basic

---
[119] Exodus 20:8-10

arithmetic and memory exercises. So, when it comes to spiritual exercise, I have a question.

When was the last time you exercised your faith? Such as,

- sharing your faith with a friend or stranger,
- praying for something very time specific and waiting to discern the answer,
- or praying for someone else, operating in a spiritual gift, prophesying, or praying for healing.

Paul writes, 'faith comes'[120], it's not an ever-present reality, we talk about standing in faith, operating in faith, like it's a conscious decision. Muscle tissue is present in your body, but you have a choice, it can either waste away or be enhanced. Got the picture? Choose to deliberately exercise your faith in the God who can do imaginably more[121]!

3. Diet

Throughout the Bible the metaphors of food and drink are used to talk about our spiritual diet.

> Then Jesus declared, 'I am the bread of life. Whoever comes to me will never go hungry, and whoever believes in me will never be thirsty.
> **John 6:35**

---

[120] Romans 10:17
[121] Ephesians 3:20-21

SCHOOL OF DISCIPLESHIP

> Jesus answered, 'It is written: "Man shall not live on bread alone, but on every word that comes from the mouth of God."'
> **Matthew 4:4**

> Jesus answered, 'Everyone who drinks this water will be thirsty again, **14** but whoever drinks the water I give them will never thirst. Indeed, the water I give them will become in them a spring of water welling up to eternal life.'
> **John 4:13-14**

> Taste and see that the LORD is good;
>   blessed is the one who takes refuge in him.
> **Psalm 34:8**

> Therefore, rid yourselves of all malice and all deceit, hypocrisy, envy, and slander of every kind. **2** Like newborn babies, crave pure spiritual milk, so that by it you may grow up in your salvation, **3** now that you have tasted that the Lord is good.
> **1 Peter 2:1-3**

Plus, many, many more. These invitations are not all about reading the Bible, but more generally feeding on God.

- Reading the Scriptures
- Meditating on the Scriptures[122]
- Studying the Scriptures

---

[122] More on this later in this chapter.

- Prayer
- Praise
- Waiting and listening on God

What's feeding us? TV programmes, boxsets, social media platforms, office gossip, celebrity culture, the next conspiracy theory, or some argumentative trending feed? Who has input into your life? And just like physical diets, there's plenty of junk food out there you need to say 'No' to.

4. Sunlight

Or should that be, *Son-light*? – ooh, cringe.

Let me tell you, during a dark season in my own spiritual walk, a time when I had let people down with inappropriate behaviour and felt disqualified from all ministry, I sensed God give me a very clear instruction – *watch Jesus and listen to what He says*.

It's a very biblical instruction, first Mary to the wedding stewards, and then the Father during the transfiguration[123]. So, I embarked on a journey that lasted eighteen months, during which time I was constantly reading through the four Gospels. I started in Luke, but the order is irrelevant, their similarities soon become apparent, especially in the Synoptics[124]. I was at a place where I was spiritually dry and suddenly had more time on my hands, and so I

---

[123] John 2:5 and Matthew 17:5

[124] The technical term that denotes the Gospels of Matthew, Mark and Luke, as they carry a clearly overlapping synopsis of the Jesus narrative.

was eager to listen to Jesus. Thankfully, I rarely suffered from the problem of overfamiliarity as I kept reading and re-reading the narratives. Bible overfamiliarity is when you see the subheading, *Parable of the Sower,* or *Feeding the Five Thousand,* and just assume you know the content and skip to something less familiar. Don't do it! God meets you in the familiar and surprises you with inspired new insights.

In the physical, humans need sunlight. There's a diagnosable condition, SAD – *seasonal affective disorder*, related to changes in the season, especially in those countries further from the equator that experience shorter and darker days.

The importance of *Sonlight*, is a spiritual reality.

> fixing our eyes on Jesus, the pioneer and perfecter of faith.
> **Hebrews 12:2**

> Since, then, you have been raised with Christ, set your hearts on things above, where Christ is, seated at the right hand of God. ² Set your minds on things above, not on earthly things.
> **Colossians 3:1-2**

Don't go a day without gazing upon Jesus – the true light of the world[125].

---
[125] John 8:12

Turn your eyes upon Jesus
Look full in His wonderful face
And the things of Earth will grow strangely dim
In the light of His glory and grace.
Copyright ©1922 Helen Howarth Lemmel, New Spring Publishing Inc.

5. Meditation

In my own lifetime this has increasingly become a broad term and a professionally accepted practice. I have an occupational therapist friend, whose team at work gather once a week for a staff meeting that includes a three-minute mindfulness exercise. Meditation is now deemed any deliberate timeout practice to refocus our thinking on something calm and healthy. As Christians we should be ahead of the game here, unfortunately we neglected this simple practice and replaced it with something far more demanding, yet apparently more (educationally) acceptable. In brief, Bible meditation, as God told Joshua to do[126], has been replaced with Bible study. Perhaps another case of the *simple*, but not necessarily *easy*, being replaced with something spiritually easier, though often requiring much more preparation time.

Let's clarify here, *both* disciplines are biblical, Bible study and Bible meditation. But they're not an 'either or', they're a 'both and'.

Here's a quick Bible meditation for you.

---

[126] Joshua 1:8

SCHOOL OF DISCIPLESHIP

Jesus said, *'I am the light of the world.'* (John 8:12).

Wow. What does that mean? What images come to mind? Perhaps Genesis 1:3, God spoke light into being, the very first words, the very first day. Before He created the sun and the moon – huh? In Matthew 5:14 Jesus said, 'you are the light of the world,' – hmm?

Is Jesus still the light of the world? If so, then how do we see that in operation in the world?

Jesus says, we're the light, so how is working through me?

The simplest of words, a single verse, or just a single phrase can provide us with at least a 3-minute break, a time to ponder, to recalibrate our spiritual instruments.

Whereas some Eastern meditation might be about emptying our minds, to free our bodies, Christian meditation is about realigning our minds with Christ. For we ought to have the mind of Christ[127].

Meditation can focus on a natural created object. A leaf. An unspoilt landscape. The rhythm of the sea. Obviously, your location may limit your choices. I know people, who once a month or every three months, deliberately choose to go to the coast, or off hiking in the hills, for the fresh air, the space and quality time

---

[127] 1 Corinthians 2:16

with God. Don't restrict yourself to unproductive routines. Use your free time wisely. Plan. Schedule. Make dates with God in your diary and honour them.

6. Supportive friendships

This is not about creating codependent relationships, where one person is like a caretaker and others take advantage of their friendship and time. Nor is it finding a mentor, strangely an increasingly popular discipleship component in recent decades[128]. Be assured, people who present themselves as a victim will most probably attract some well-intentioned people around them. This is not that! Those are not supportive friendships.

This is about finding people, who treat you as an equal, where mutual support is given. Where the conversation isn't all about you. It's about life, fun, laughter and of course – God! A place where honesty resides, allowing for vulnerability and transparency.

There is a problem, sadly. Having witnessed hundreds of people over the years during my church-based ministry, these mutual and trustworthy relationships can't be manufactured. If they're clinically pursued, they become overly functional and lopsided. Such skewed relationships will default inevitably to a level of co-dependency, and eventual disappointment due to unfulfilled

---

[128] I'm not against the wise and productive use of a mentor. Though I am intrigued how many young people are longing for this person-type in their lives – or does this say more about our society, insecurities and the need for regular handholding?

expectations. When the purely functional or clinical reality of the relationship becomes apparent, it will breakdown, causing feelings of rejection to emerge. Rejection begets rejection, with the victim often initiating the collapse, in order to avoid the inevitable perceived personal rejection. It's a casebook scenario, not at all uncommon, yet still a painful reality for both parties involved, until healing can be suggested, initiated and ministered.

Answers? I've met dozens of individuals who have literally asked me to my face to find them friends in the church. Not a mentor. Not a pastorally-wise person to confide in – but to go out there and produce friends for them. The fact they say that, means it's not going to work. Interesting fact, it's equally true of the dozens of people I've met desperate for the Holy Spirit, they long for that real and tangible experience of God's presence – but again, it rarely happens for such people. Healthy relationships require chemistry, and part of that chemistry is the ability to relax and be yourself with one another, and not to hide some alternative agenda. We need to learn to sit with God without Him having to answer our perceived pressing needs. Learn to sit in peace, knowing you're loved and treasured. Simple? But for many it's not easy – that's for sure.

I take the relational nature of Christianity very seriously. You may have already guessed that. Therefore, if someone really struggles in forming social relationships, then I am also concerned about the reality, breadth and genuine depth of their daily walk with Christ. Jesus had amazing social skills, The Gospels show Him engaging with a breadth of people, being compassionate, merciful, realistic and honest. He also experienced true rejection, time and again, but His identity was so rooted in His Father, even when questioning the loyalty of the Twelve[129], He was not shaken.

Once I had a neighbour's cat who would often wander into our garden. He'd jump on my lap, or just curl up on an adjacent garden chair. Other house guests, when spotting the cat would call for his attention. They'd even pick him up and park him on their lap or squeeze him between themselves and the arm of a chair. He'd hiss, bare his teeth and jump free. No one likes manipulation.

I can't help you make friends. It either comes naturally, or not. Three possible suggestions for those struggling.

1. Talk to people – obviously! But don't target people or prioritise them based on unhelpful criteria: their importance, their looks, their popularity. Talk to a breadth of people and see where things just 'click'.
2. Listen to people, show genuine interest in them by asking them questions.
3. Avoid deliberately turning conversations to your agenda.
4. Say 'Yes' when invited to lunch or a small group meeting. If someone reaches out to you, then be open and generous with your time.

---
[129] John 6:67

My first wife was an introvert[130]. Low self-esteem in her teens led to some unhealthy learnt defensive behaviour. Though her Christian faith started to change some of these characteristics. The same thing happened to me, within a year of becoming a Christian my extrovert tendencies started to emerge from an unnatural emotionally stifling background.

Christianity is corporate, church ought to function as a community. Trust God in this, He knows what He's doing. I've known dozens of introverts who can function socially, better than most extroverts as they're often far more aware of the value and purpose of being together. My late wife eventually became a manager in her job, then a lecturer at a theological college and a regular Bible teacher and preacher. She never became an extrovert. She simply took responsibility within the corporate to function using her gifts, wisdom and life experiences.

To conclude
So, there you have it, the six universal keys to a healthier life, as seen through a pair of spirit-filled glasses. Practical and simple,

---

[130] Distinguishing introverts from extroverts has far more to do with learning styles and how individuals prefer to process information than presumed characteristics or behaviour. For example, shyness is often linked to insecurities. For an introvert, being shy is quite easy, it demands little response. For the extrovert, such insecurities are overcompensated thus often projecting an uncomfortable lack of self-awareness. Our cognitive preferences should not rob us of a corporate existence or be used as an excuse to deny the group our specific skills and insights.

though not necessarily easy. Have a go. Change your routine. Change your priorities. Engage increasingly with God and God's people. If you start tomorrow, mark it in your diary and after 28 days gently assess your progress, or your failings, or a mix of both. But don't wait 28 days[131] to make obvious adjustments. Learn to steer a new course, and how to navigate the occasional squall. Learn. Grow. Become spiritually confident. Become a holistic and effective disciple of Jesus.

---

[131] They say it takes 28 days to form a habit or to break a habit. Hence UK mental health sectioning is often 28 days, and the Sandra Bullock movie of the same title about addiction. As Jesus said, as disciples, we need to put our hand to the plough and not look back (Luke 9:62), actually His words were much sterner than that if you dare to look it up.

1 John 2:6

Whoever claims to live in him must live as Jesus did.

CHAPTER 5

Becoming More Jesus

LEARNING OUTCOMES | To examine aspects of *The Sermon on the Mount* to discover Jesus's heart and agenda in order to become more Christ-centred and Kingdom-focussed in our discipleship.

The three chapters of Matthew 5, 6 & 7 are commonly called *The Sermon on the Mount*. They present a summary of Christ's expectations for any who would follow Him. The teaching is practical, spiritual, encouraging and challenging. It's pretty much Jesus's own *School of Discipleship*.

Although the entire sermon only appears in Matthew's Gospel, many of its smaller components are edited into Luke's Gospel. There's no reason to doubt that Jesus shared *The Sermon on the Mount* in one sitting, and then continued to reference parts of it at different times throughout His public ministry. Most *teaching-preachers* do the same, no matter the subject at hand, they will invariably pull-on their core values and weave these into their public ministry. I know I do. There's also an American pastor, who will remain nameless, who has authored several books. The overlap (or repetition) of material in each new publication could cause me as a *consumer* to feel cheated, but as a *disciple*, learning from a man of spiritual wisdom, I'm comforted that his biblical vision and key foundational truths remain consistent – the repetition in this context actually speaks to his integrity[132].

Let's turn our thinking to Matthew 5-7. There is a significant structure to *The Sermon on the Mount* that reflects its time and culture. In the West, we are used to linear arguments which build a case one point after another, leading to a conclusion. In the Ancient Near East, they had a more circular approach to teaching. Where the crux of a matter would be located in the middle of their words. The opening statements would present the case, leading to a central revelation or challenge, which then led (logically) to the application. I'm aware this textual information may not be particularly interesting to everyone, but bear with me for another paragraph or so.

Consider Paul's letters to the various churches. They generally end with very specific, even named, instructions. Romans, Ephesians,

---

[132] I hope you will take the same gracious approach when I repeat myself in this publication and refer to the same Bible texts on more than one occasion.

and Colossians are all examples of this. In the Book of Romans, the opening chapters are full of intense theology based around the Law and the work of Christ. Chapter 8 talks about our changed identity, heirs with the Father, co-heirs with the Son, and the work of the Spirit within us. Later, in chapter 12, the application mode begins in full swing, with a powerful opening challenge,

> Therefore, I urge you, brothers and sisters, in view of God's mercy, to offer your bodies as a living sacrifice, holy and pleasing to God—this is your true and proper worship. ² Do not conform to the pattern of this world, but be transformed by the renewing of your mind. Then you will be able to test and approve what God's will is—his good, pleasing and perfect will.
> **Romans 12:1-2**

Another example is Paul's letter to the Ephesians. The two halves come together in chapter 4,

> I urge you to live a life worthy of the calling you have received.
> **Ephesians 4:!b**

Prior to this verse Paul has reminded the church (extensively) of the work of Christ, as he moves to application, the motivation is to live a life worthy of our calling – worthy of all Christ has done for us.

Alternatively, as an exception to prove the rule, 1 Corinthians is a letter deliberately responding to specific questions the church has asked, and so each chapter break roughly coincides with a different subject matter.

Applying this ancient textual structure to Matthew 5-7, we will discover at the heart of *The Sermon on the Mount*, is a classic paragraph, often referred to as *The Lord's Prayer*[133]. Here, in less than sixty words, Jesus summaries the heart of His mission, including the relational nature of God and His continuing grace towards us. This is the *Christ manifesto* for all disciples, captured in the form of a memorable prayer.

1. Praise – the focus is on God, yet with the amazing intimacy to call Him, Father, whilst still honouring His heavenly presence
2. Purpose – it's all about His Kingdom and His will manifesting on Earth as in Heaven. That's quite a task.
3. Provision – daily bread, representing daily needs.
4. Pardon – the asking for, and offering of, forgiveness.
5. Protection – from the evil one's schemes
6. Praise 2 – from the traditional longer liturgical ending, *Yours is the Kingdom, the power and the glory. Amen.*[134]

---

[133] Matthew 6:9-13

[134] To explain the longer ending of the Lord's Prayer, common within the Protestant tradition would take a separate essay. The words are found in the 1611 King James Bible based on the Byzantian Greek Texts, but the later discovered and assumed more accurate Alexandrian Texts don't have the longer ending. Scholarship, based on the evidence, is undecided. The *Didache* a first century document dated around 90AD contains the additional words, so the longer prayer, as we know it, was used very early in our church tradition. The words themselves are clearly biblical, echoing the language

BECOMING MORE JESUS

We could just stop there, six succinct prayerful statements. Anything else would simply be expanding on these essential foundations. Though granted, the subject of God's Kingdom is vast and when understood, should permeate every aspect of our lives, like yeast being worked into the whole of the dough[135]. Even Jesus used many parables to help enhance His Kingdom teaching. For the sake of clarity, the Kingdom of God[136] can be summarised into three dynamic components.

1. Reformation – *Kingdom ethics.* God's expectations for our life choices, how we choose to behave, and His moral code for interacting with others. We see this demonstrated in Christ's compassion toward the marginalised, and those society has pre-judged. In the Luke 10 mission when He commissions the seventy(-two), guidelines concerning hospitality is one of the first instructions.
2. Transformation – *Kingdom power.* Jesus came to disarm the enemy, expel demons and bring holistic and lasting healing

---

of David's prayer from 1 Chronicles 29:11-13. So, did Jesus say these words? We don't know. But could He have said these words? Undoubtedly, yes!

[135] Matthew 13:33

[136] In Matthew's Gospel, the *Kingdom of God* is often referred to as the *Kingdom of Heaven*. It's thought that Matthew was writing to a primarily Jewish audience, due to his increased use of the Hebrew Scriptures in the text and the extensive genealogy in chapter 1. With this in mind, the holiness of God's name to the Jews, often translated *Adonai* (LORD) in the Old Testament, is replaced in the Gospel with the word *Heaven*. Though this can lead to a misunderstanding of the phrase, there's no evidence that Matthew is referring to anything different than the *Kingdom of God* referenced in the other Synoptics and less frequently in John.

– even unto everlasting life. In Luke 10, the Kingdom mission clearly involved healings.
3. Proclamation – *Kingdom teaching*. This includes the parables and all Christ's wise sayings and comments/instruction upon everyday life. Interestingly in Luke 10:1-9, this aspect of the 'gospel' is the final stage of Christ's missional strategy.

All of this can be summed up in two words – *Good News*[137]. Good news for all, especially the poor, the broken-hearted, the ones held captive to their behavioural choices; God is announcing freedom, deliverance and favour[138].

The Kingdom of God in Scripture does not denote a geographical realm, like the United Kingdom, but wherever God's rule and reign is evident. It's detected in a miracle or an exorcism, these power encounters reveal the presence of God's Kingdom

> But if I [Jesus] drive out demons by the finger of God, then the kingdom of God has come upon you.
> **Luke 11:20**

---

137 Mark 1:15. The Greek word *euaggelion* literally means good news or good tidings. The Anglo-Saxon word is *god-spell*, meaning, a good story – i.e. good news.

[138] In Luke 4:18, Jesus is quoting from Isaiah 61. Here proclamation is mentioned first or is then re-interpreted through significant reforming and transforming acts. When asked if He was the One, Jesus replied by referring to His miracles (Matthew 11:4-5). Francis of Assisi (1181-1226) is often quoted to have said, "share the Gospel at all times, and if necessary, use words." Annoyingly, factchecking this leads us to the conclusion that neither he nor any of his immediate disciples used such a memorable phrase. Though the following words are authentically his, "Start by doing what is necessary, then what is possible, and suddenly you are doing the impossible."

BECOMING MORE JESUS

However, it's clear by looking at the world, God is not reigning supreme in all righteousness. The Kingdom is best likened to light piercing darkness, and more appropriately the dawn of a new day[139]. This 'now and not yet' reality of the Kingdom is called eschatological tension – literally a tension between now and the final end time victory. We live in the end times. In Luke 4:19, Jesus is quoting from Isaiah 61:2. He seems to deliberately stop after declaring *the year of the Lord's favour*, choosing not to talk about *the day of God's vengeance*. His message is primarily *good* news, the attraction of the Kingdom now, which should outweigh fears of a coming judgment. Church history has an alternative record, where the Kingdom has almost been ignored and edited out from a new message that plays on people's fear and a hellish future of eternal conscious torment. Returning to Isaiah's original words, compare one day of God's wise and final judgement, to three hundred and sixty-five days of His transformational blessings. Do the maths, a year is considerably longer than a single day! Since that first Pentecost outpouring in Acts 2, the church remains in the end times, a period that is marked out by the generous outpouring and anointing of the Holy Spirit upon all peoples, young and old, male and female; and the promise, that if anyone

---

[139] Malachi 4:2, the *sun of righteousness will rise with healing in its rays,* language depicting a dawning of miracles. This image was used by Charles Wesley in *Hark! The Hearld Angels Sing*, though it is often changed to 'son of righteousness' either out of ignorance or to bring clarity to the imagery.

Sermon on the Mount structure and distinctives

I love that Jesus begins His message with blessings[141]. The word can be translated 'happy' or even, 'lucky are you', though today that would be deemed inappropriate language by most Christians.

Jesus deliberately speaks encouragement. No matter what the situation, no matter how grave the circumstances, we are happy – because the Kingdom of God is evident. God reminds us He is personable (relational), we're called His children, we're told we can actually see God. We are now the 'lights of the world', the 'salt of the earth'. It's a great motivational opener – and of course, there's no spin, it's all true![142]

How many sermons have you heard that start by declaring happiness, blessings and favour over your life? Jesus does it eight times over and continues by giving us titles of influence and significance[143]. Amid one of the cruellest occupations, with its unpredictable arrests, enslavements and death, Jesus speaks blessings and significance. If you're a preacher – take note!

---

[140] Acts 2:17-21, quoting from Joel 2:28-32.
[141] Matthew 5:3-12
[142] Read Matthew 5:1-16 to discover these truths for yourself.
[143] Peacemakers and children of God (5:9), the salt of the earth (5:13), light of the word (5:14).

Jesus's sermon continues concerning the ethics of His Kingdom. These are not quite the same as the written Law. God is fulfilling the old by raising the standards for the new. *Simple* to read, not necessarily *easy* to live.

After the opening blessings, our new identity and purpose, comes the heightened need for godly living, followed by the central matter of investing in our personal spirituality, where Jesus highlights giving, praying and fasting. Then we move to some direct instructions, such as, stop judging others, remember you're a work in progress too. Therefore, do unto others, as you would want them to do to you. In summary, listen to God's wisdom and put it into practise. To conclude, build as a wise builder. Read Matthew 5-7, to discover these highlights for yourself and some I may have neglected.

Spiritual banking

In Matthew 6, at the centre of the sermon, which is, Hebraically, at a point of great significance, Jesus talks about acts of righteousness, specifically naming, giving, praying and fasting. So, we have three explicit Jesus-given disciplines to help the formation of our lives to align to His Kingdom. At the end of the chapter, we're told not to worry about the everyday, but to seek first God's Kingdom and His righteousness. Therefore, the purpose of discipleship is quite clear, to nurture spiritual disciplines in order to be increasingly Kingdom aware, and less distracted by life's routines. Yet, interestingly, at this point in the sermon as we seek to pursue God, we encounter two words from the lips of Jesus that are, on the whole, deemed inappropriate in most Christian environments today: *secrets* and *rewards*.

> But when you give to the needy, do not let your left hand know what your right hand is doing, [4] so that your giving may be in secret. Then your Father, who sees what is done in secret, will reward you.
>
> Then your Father, who sees what is done in secret, will reward you.
>
> and your Father, who sees what is done in secret, will reward you.
> **Matthew 6: 3-4, 6 & 18**

Secrets are normally seen as unhelpful things to have in our lives. Often the enemy lurks in the unhealthy secrets of others. In pastoral ministry the word is sometimes attached to a person's bad habit, their *secret sin*, an embarrassing flaw that they can't tell anyone else about.

In the context of Christ's words, He's not talking about some clandestine information we must keep to ourselves, but spiritual behaviour that can only be nurtured at a personal level. Earlier, I mentioned the corporate nature of Hebraic thought, being aware of others and serving people are important components in any form of community life; however, the relational nature of our walk with God requires personal evidence of our devotion. These are things that we don't parade in public but nurture in private, such as our financial generosity, prayer and fasting.

As evangelical believers, we proclaim a Gospel of grace. Salvation cannot be earned, it's an undeserved gift from God, made available through the sacrifice of Jesus. So, as Christians we rarely talk of receiving rewards, because our theology often deems our 'good works' as worthless. Salvation is by grace alone, lest anyone boast in their own works[144]. However, in our restored relationship with God, we are told that as His handiwork, we were created to do His good works[145]. Works that have nothing to do with our salvation but reveal our obedience and commitment to our new calling in Christ Jesus. Importantly, there's more to this, which is often overlooked, for in our obedience, God speaks of rewards. Who doesn't like to get a reward?

We probably know the story of David and Goliath? The little shepherd boy with his slingshot who took down the giant Philistine warrior. Read the narrative again, there's more to it than David turning up to defeat the infidel. For some time, King Saul has been seeking a brave challenger, and the successful victor would win the hand of his daughter in marriage and they and their family would be exempt from paying any more tax[146]. Funny we often miss the relevance of these statements, which are deliberately repeated in the text and talked about for clarity

---

[144] Ephesians 2:8-9
[145] Ephesians 2:10
[146] 1 Samuel 17:25

among the Hebrew soldiers[147]. Humanity hasn't changed, we love to be motivated by rewards, and God knows that. Perhaps it's part of our 'in His image' creation.

> For the joy that was set before him he endured the cross, scorning its shame, and sat down at the right hand of the throne of God.
> **Hebrews 12:2**

I do not want to make light of the Cross and Christ's horrific suffering and sacrifice. But why did Jesus in his wrestling in Gethsemane, even unto sweating blood[148], submit to His Father's will? Was it purely the clinical decision to be an obedient son, or were the pragmatic results of His sacrifice motivating His decision even unto death?

So, let's clarified secrets and rewards one more time. In the context of Matthew 6, secrets are to be understood as the private disciplines within our Christian walk. The promised rewards are the benefits that arise from the consistency of our discipleship, they are byproducts of God's salvation, not some form of winnings that count towards our salvation. Now we have that straight, let me introduce you to the concept of *spiritual banking*.

> 'Do not store up for yourselves treasures on earth, where moths and vermin destroy, and where thieves break in and

---

[147] 1 Samuel 17:26-27. They had just told David in verse 25, but he asks again in verse 26, and so in verse 27 they repeat the rewards.
[148] Luke 22:44

> steal. **20** But store up for yourselves treasures in heaven, where moths and vermin do not destroy, and where thieves do not break in and steal. **21** For where your treasure is, there your heart will be also.
> **Matthew 6:19-21**

Immediately after Jesus talks of secrets and rewards, He expressly tells us not to gather our possessions here on Earth, where they can be eroded away, but in heaven. So, we need to open a celestial bank account for safe keeping. This is the place where my Christian spiritual experiences of breakthroughs, answers to prayer, the personal maturity developed through fasting, and the wisdom, faith and joy you receive when ministering to others[149]. I believe that somehow our Christian disciplines and acts of righteousness are converted into lasting Kingdom currency and put on deposit for future withdrawals.

On the occasion when Jesus said of a demon's expulsion, that this sort does not come out without prayer and fasting[150], I'm not convinced that the context lends itself to imply we need to say a special prayer whilst fasting to do deliverance ministry. Otherwise, when faced with someone's need that requires an exorcism, you may have to quietly apologise, if you've already had breakfast. Or say, come back after lunch, so you have the opportunity to skip the meal in order to fast. This approach would be ludicrous. The power of prayer in our lives is not rooted alone in the very words

---

[149] Acts 20:35, these are said to be the words of Jesus, though they're not recorded in the Gospels, where a *blessing* is attached to our service.
[150] Mark 9:29, the reference to *fasting* doesn't appear in all the manuscripts.

we speak at a set time, but the lifestyle of prayer we've been nurturing. The real encouragement in Jesus's words here about prayer and fasting, regards the power we acquire for effective ministry through the ongoing disciplines of prayer and fasting in our lives. It's like we're 'banking' our Christian faithfulness and commitment, so when needed, for a power encounter, we can make a legitimate withdrawal.

In Acts 19 we encounter the rather bizarre account of some people trying to copy Paul's ministry and as a consequence they suffered badly at the hands of some demons – for attempting to make an illegitimate withdrawal[151].

These words make it clear,

> They triumphed over him
>   by the blood of the Lamb
>   and by the word of their testimony;
> they did not love their lives so much
>   as to shrink from death.
> **Revelation 12:11**

Our ability to triumph over the enemy is twofold. The victory of Jesus through His death, *and* the words of our testimony. That is the genuineness of our discipleship, even unto death. Sobering words indeed. The devil will not be fooled, our hypocrisy will not go unnoticed.

---

[151] Acts 19:13-16

Therefore, the genuineness and faithfulness of our everyday spiritual walk, brings spiritual confidence to our future ministry. Of course, the metaphor of *spiritual banking* breaks down if we only view it in monetary or legally quantifiable terms. Perhaps, four hours of prayer and two missed meals gives you a parking space at a busy time of the day. One hundred hours of worship, involving three days of fasting – and you can cast out a demon. Nonsense! *Spiritual banking* is not formulaic, it is simply the consequence of having a genuine and consistent relationship with God. Like any relationship, the more confidence you gain around each other the more risks you can take. Good friends can both be honest and sarcastic with each other. Take the example of John, the disciple of Jesus who knew he was loved. Therefore, it was he who was urged by the others to ask Jesus which of the disciples would betray Him[152]. Perhaps they asked John because he and his brother had already had the front to ask Jesus for the best seats

> The more quality time we spend with God, the more confident we become in our relationship to see God at work – that's discipleship!

---

[152] John 13:23-24

in heaven[153]. Then, when Jesus declined their request, they got their mum to ask the same question[154]. The more quality time we spend with God, the more confident we become in our relationship to see God at work – that's discipleship!

Consider the example of Jesus. He rose early in the morning to escape the crowds to have time in prayer, then later in the day while ministering He would state that He only did what He saw the Father doing[155]. He wasn't formulaically cashing in hours of prayer for miracles, He was forever growing in confidence in discerning His Father's work. For us it's about nurturing a spiritual lifestyle that gives us greater clarity in having the mind of Christ[156]. Matthew 6 talks of three acts of righteousness, giving, prayer and fasting. I'm not convinced these three disciplines are the only ones we need to invest in. Though the three referenced by Jesus do serve as examples of how religion can manipulate these disciplines into something very public and showy. In politics we know that generous contributions come with strings attached. Similarly, wordy public prayers (or even sharing a prophecy) could be seen as a way of saying – 'Hey, listen to how spiritual I am.' True fasting never requires a screwed-up face, bad breath, and pious statements like, 'Oh, no cake for me, I'm fasting.'

---

[153] Mark 10:35-37
[154] Matthew 20:20-21
[155] John 5:19
[156] 1 Corinthians 2:16

BECOMING MORE JESUS

A side note on long wordy prayers. Sometimes we need to lend our voice (and vocabulary) to shame the schemes of the evil one and to clearly declare the purposes of God, in order to see the breakthrough we're longing for. I've endured some wordy prayers in my time and only spiritual discernment helps to clarify their effectiveness in the context of spiritual warfare.

The Lord's Prayer is very comprehensive with an amazing economy of words. Better still, I love these examples from Jesus,

- Be quiet! – Mark 1:25, and a demon is expelled.
- Be clean! – Mark 1:41, and leper is cured
- Quiet! Be still! – Mark 4:39, and even the waves and wind obey Him

I think these serve as examples of spiritual banking withdrawals, there's no lengthy pleading of your cause, just the *simple* confidence that God's got this covered within the integrity of your words.

I've learnt, when directly addressing the demonic – less is more. It sort of makes sense, if you're speaking with the spiritual authority of Christ, backed up with the witness of your own day-to-day life, then your prayers will overcome the enemy.

We're told to store up treasure in heaven, Matthew 6:20. Heaven is not a future concept, heaven is a present reality, an active place, not purely a final destination, it is also the present home of your unspoilt riches. There's a cliché, couples who pray together, stay together. What makes one marriage stronger than another? Well, probably nothing that is deliberately on display in public, but the quiet assurances, respect, love and honouring of one another away from the gaze of others. Likewise, in your relationship with God, your personal secret (non-public) disciplines strengthen your confidence with God – now that's a great reward and a great motivation.

To continue with the metaphor, I can personally make withdrawals from my spiritual banking, such as praying prayers of extraordinary faith, but normally these 'withdrawals' are relational, it's because I'm responding to what I'm discerning the Father is doing – sounds familiar, John 5:19. Out of compassion I'll happily pray for anyone presenting themselves with a need. Yet, now and again, I get a Spirit-led conviction to pray with unshakeable certainty about specific situations. As I recall examples of this, I'm reminded of one of the first miracles I witnessed, as we prayed against an imminent miscarriage. In my faith-filled declarations I used the Scripture of the woman who pushed through the crowds to receive her healing[157], we prayed for the bleeding to stop – and it did. Another example was a woman, who for two years had been unable to walk unassisted. We prayed for her on a Sunday morning. Now in this situation, many of us had all prayed before on several previous occasions, however, but on this specific morning a number of prophetic words, the faith of the woman in

---

[157] Mark 5:25-29

question, and a fresh unction for a miracle, all coincided producing a faith-filled room of great expectation. We prayed. Nothing happened. But the following morning, to her own surprise, she swung out of bed and walked!

In faithfulness and compassion, we need to pray whenever asked. Yet now and again, spiritual discernment kicks in, and our inner spirit is stirred by the Spirit of God with increased faith[158].

In regards *spiritual banking*, though I can teach and share my experiences to encourage others, I cannot make a significant deposit into your own account. I can give insights on how I personally pray, fast, witness, worship, etc. I can even pray prayers of impartation. Timothy received such a deposit, and later Paul reminded him[159] that he had an account with God already open. Well, not in so many words, but I believe in impartation[160] as an initiation into the next field of ministry. Nevertheless, nothing can replace your own personal investments with God.

Remember, discipleship is relational. Becoming more Jesus begins by spending more time with His Father.

---

[158] Perhaps this the gift of faith listed in 1 Corinthians 12:9
[159] 2 Timothy 1:6
[160] Romans 1:11

Colossians 2:6-7

So then, just as you received Christ Jesus as Lord, continue to live your lives in him, ⁷ rooted and built up in him, strengthened in the faith as you were taught, and overflowing with thankfulness.

CHAPTER 6

Thanksgiving

LEARNING OUTCOMES | To move the notion of prayer away from personal petitions, to discover the value of thanksgiving and praise.

Traditional discipleship often puts an emphasis on Bible reading and prayer. In my ministry I've learnt that praise and thanksgiving are truly essential spiritual tools for our development and survival. Often seen as emotional and subjective, they're easily dismissed as optional preferences but not mandatory. I beg to differ, Psalm 100 is clear, we are to enter God's presence with thanksgiving and draw close in praise[161]. Never start a time of corporate worship with confession. It may seem logical, however, confession rarely brings us closer to God, as its focus is on our mistakes, therefore

---

[161] Psalm 100:4

we end up thinking about ourselves and God becomes distant due to the increased awareness of our failings. Thanksgiving and praise puts the focus on God. Irrespective of our feelings or pressing issues, God is God and is worthy of our praise. In Colossians 3, Paul calls us to holiness in terms of removing obvious destructive and addictive sins from our lives[162]. However, first, and most importantly, he begins by getting us to look above to where Christ is seated[163].

The apostle Paul knew that conversion and discipleship were two different things. In encountering God personally, the problems of the old life can be resolved as our new life emerges. For Paul this is a done deal[164], though he's also clearly aware that this scenario can often define some Christians for years, as the old is never truly crucified, thus restricting the new believer from finding freedom and maturity. Paul talks of changing our clothes[165], changing our vantage point[166], having escaped the darkness[167] and walking as children of light[168]. And of course, the inevitable garden analogy, of being rooted in our newfound faith and growing.

> So then, just as you received Christ Jesus as Lord, continue to live your lives in him, rooted and built up in him, strengthened

---

[162] Colossians 3:5-14, it's an extensive passage.
[163] Colossians 3:1
[164] 2 Corinthians 5:17
[165] Ephesians 4:22-23
[166] Colossians 3:1 (as just stated, earlier)
[167] Colossians 1:13
[168] Ephesians 5:8

THANKSGIVING

> in the faith as you were taught, and overflowing with thanksgiving.
> **Colossians 2:6-7**

In *The Grace* (2 Corinthians 13:14), we looked briefly at Jesus's threefold title, *Lord Jesus Christ*. Here in Colossians 2, Paul separates out the components, stressing that Jesus was more than just the expected messianic figure, but actually God come to Earth He is the *Lord*. Paul uses the same emphasis in Philippians 2:11, after a celebration of the incarnation, submission, obedience and sacrifice of Jesus, every tongue will confess, and every knee will bow acknowledging Jesus Christ as *Lord*. To grow in God, we need to both acknowledge and embrace Christ's Lordship. King David put it clearly and simply.

> The Lord is my Shepherd, I shall want for nothing.
> **Psalm 23:1**

If Jesus is purely a historical figure, we can endlessly debate the value and morality of His teachings. If He was only the Christ, anointed on a mission as the Saviour of the World, then the blessings of eternal life are all ours at the cruel expense of His sufferings and sacrifice. Yet He was even more than that, He is the Word, that was there in the beginning, become flesh, God Himself in human form[169]. Already all of heaven is acknowledging, rejoicing and praising the Lamb upon the throne, as the Lion of

---

[169] John 1:1-14

SCHOOL OF DISCIPLESHIP

Judah, the King of kings and Lord of lords[170]. Jesus Christ is LORD, and as such, is endlessly worthy of our praise and thanksgiving.

James warns us that the tongue, such a small part of our body has the power to wreak havoc. Don't embrace hypocrisy by allowing your tongue to carry both curses and blessings[171]. Jesus was clear, the mouth speaks from what overflows from our heart[172]. Therefore, if your mouth is full of honest praise, it's much harder for your mind to be simultaneously full of anger or negative thoughts. If God inhabit the praises of His people[173], then who is inhabiting our negativity and unchecked criticisms? They say, a healthy body a healthy mind. It's true. It's Hebraic, our body, soul and spirit are inseparably linked. Praise God and find reasons to be thankful, and your life, general perceptions and physical countenance will change for the better.

To understand more about biblical praise and the powerful dynamics of Christ-centred worship read my book, **School of Praise.** I don't want to regurgitate the insights of that publication here. So, if you want to go deeper, the option is there. Otherwise, in brief, the simplicity of this discipline is to nurture a prayer language of thankfulness and praise. Simple? Though not always easy.

---

[170] Revelation 5:5, 9-14 & 17:14
[171] James 3:5 & 10
[172] Matthew 12:34b
[173] Psalm 22:3, explicit in the KJV, strongly suggested in the NASB.

THANKSGIVING

Right now, wherever you are. Stop. Now, think of three things you're thankful for, and acknowledge God's faithfulness in those things. Can you do that?

If you're really struggling,

1. Jesus says, if any of you are tired or heavy burdened come to me and I will give you rest[174]. Nice!
2. Again, He says, how much more will your Heavenly Father give the Holy Spirit to those who ask?[175] So ask!
3. Paul writes, whatever is true, noble, right, pure, praiseworthy think of these things[176], that is, change the focus of your thoughts, look unto Jesus, the author and perfector of your life[177].

Become thankful. Even in the midst of ongoing unresolved issues, turn your eyes upon Jesus. *Simple*, but not necessarily *easy*. Use Psalm 100, better still use the contents of Psalm 34. I've often presented this Psalm as a challenge. It goes like this, read Psalm 34 out loud (that's important) twice through, perhaps even three times – your emotional wellbeing will improve. Go on, have a go, and prove me wrong if you can.

---

[174] Matthew 11:28-30
[175] Luke 11:13
[176] Philippians 4:8
[177] Hebrews 12:2

SCHOOL OF DISCIPLESHIP

This chapter is deliberately short. What more can I say? Along with the disciplines of Bible reading and prayer, that can sometimes become mechanical and self-orientated; invest in bring a sacrifice of praise through genuine thanksgiving, a discipline that will help keep your eyes on God.

> Through Jesus, therefore, let us continually offer to God a sacrifice of praise – the fruit of lips that openly profess his name.
> **Hebrews 13:15**

> Rejoice always, [17] pray continually, [18] give thanks in all circumstances; for this is God's will for you in Christ Jesus.
> **1 Thessalonians 5:16-18**

Enough said.

THANKSGIVING

1 Corinthians 12:4-6

There are different kinds of gifts, but the same Spirit distributes them. There are different kinds of service, but the same Lord. There are different kinds of working, but in all of them and in everyone it is the same God at work.

CHAPTER 7

Gifts Gifts Gifts

LEARNING OUTCOMES | To briefly unpack the New Testament gifts of the Holy Spirit provided to empower and equip us for Kingdom ministry.

It would be odd to have a book promoting bicycle rides around the Yorkshire Dales without an opening chapter or a final appendix on the basics of bicycle maintenance. In this book I've placed an emphasis on fellowship with the Holy Spirit, including an entire chapter about keeping in step with the Spirit, therefore we need to examine a little more closely the work of the Holy Spirit.

The Holy Spirit ministers and equips us in a number of ways. Here's an easy to remember alliteration.

- **Power** – the word used by Jesus in Acts 1:8, for the purpose of the promised Holy Spirit is to empower us for ministry. It's one of three words Paul uses to encourage the timid Timothy to embrace the Spirit's anointing on his life, for the Spirit brings *power, love and self-discipline*[178].
- **Purity** – to be sanctified. Letting the peace and message of Christ wash over us[179]. Though our sins have been forgiven our newfound faith needs to be exercised and our new saintly identity needs touching up from time to time as we live in a less than holy world with its distractions and enticements. Paul encourages us:

> Don't get drunk with wine... Instead, be [continually] filled with the Spirit.
> **Ephesians 5:18** [adding 'continually' denotes the original tense and purpose of the verb.]

- **Presence** – this is often assumed (because God is omnipresent), and therefore, often dismissed as subjective, when we're encouraged to *invite* His presence, *welcome* His presence, *sense* His presence. There are times when God's Spirit turns up[180] and times when He seems absent from

---

[178] 2 Timothy 1:7, *self-discipline* can also be translated as *self-control* or having a *sound mind* or *good judgment*.
[179] 1 Thessalians 4:23 & Colossians 3:15-16
[180] Acts 4:31, a fresh intensity and infilling of His presence.

GIFTS GIFTS GIFTS

believers[181]. The Holy Spirit is a person[182] not a mechanism, therefore His presence is relational, and can be affected by prayer, presenting needs and open hearts.

Earlier we looked at length at the fruit of the Spirit, with a fresh emphasis on fellowshipping with the Holy Spirit rather than earnestly seeking to cultivate individual fruits in our lives. Now we'll look at the gifts God has provided for His church in a similar way. Like anyone showering their beloved with gifts, any list of these gifts should be treated as partial, never able to fully capture God's generosity toward His children. Like the nine fruit of Galatians 5:22-23, the nine gifts listed in 1 Corinthians 12 have undoubtedly been over emphasised and analysed. Indeed, read to the end of chapter 12 and Paul starts to mention additional gifts. Compare them to the five (or four) listed in Ephesians 4:11, and you'll discover it's not a perfect match. Now throw into the mix Romans 12, and if you were to create a Venn diagram of the four lists found in these three different chapters, the only one that appears all four times is, prophecy. Perhaps that's why Paul writes,

> Follow the way of love and eagerly desire gifts of the Spirit, especially prophecy.
> **1 Corinthians 14:1**

Three mini commands in one verse,

---

[181] Acts 8:15-16 & 19:2-3
[182] Able to be grieved (Ephesians 4:30) and quenched (1 Thessalonians 5:19).

SCHOOL OF DISCIPLESHIP

1. The priority to *love*.
2. *Earnestly desire*, the Greek word is linked to coveting. Wow! A concept that is a definite no-no in the Ten Commandments regarding your neighbour's ass[183], indeed regarding your neighbour – full stop. But here, Paul pulls on this carnal desire and redeems it from its original negativity when placed in the context of deliberately pursuing God's supernatural gifts. Do you covet the gifts? How do show God that you earnestly desire them?
3. *Especially the gift of prophecy*. This makes biblical sense,
    i. The greatest commandment is love (note 1 Corinthians 14:1's opening phrase) loving God and the second is like it, love everyone else[184].
    ii. Prophecy is a Holy Spirit inspired gift specifically for the edification of others[185].

Perhaps it's this emphasis on prophecy, in all three of Paul's letters, that led me to write the **School of Prophecy** book. I can't summarise here what is contained in that much larger comprehensive volume. In brief, the New Testament gift of prophecy is sharing that 'thing' that you discern God has brought to mind. It's as simple as that. Link this with Paul's sound advice in 1 Corinthians 14:3, that prophecy is spoken to others for their *strengthening, encouragement and comfort*, which means, if you didn't quite discern accurately, you can't bring about any real

---

[183] Exodus 20:17
[184] Matthew 22:37-40
[185] 1 Corinthians 14:3

harm if the intention was to bless. Anyway, you're allowed to get it wrong! The New Testament says so[186]. To know more and to learn how to safely activate the gift within you and others, read the **School of Prophecy**.

Gifts gifts gifts

Why the threefold title? Why the repetition? For the benefit of your discipleship, it may help to recognise the possible differences in the three passages mentioned earlier.

The classic starting place is 1 Corinthians 12, even though the phrase spiritual gifts doesn't appear in the Greek text. Paul uses two words as he introduces the subject, *charismata* literally meaning a gift of grace, and *pneumatica*, something spiritual or of the Spirit. In English translations these two words are brought together to form the notion of spiritual gifts. Sadly, the emphasis in the original Greek is lost in our English understanding. With the emphasis on *gift*, we naturally perceive these supernatural abilities are given for our possession; like a gift – once received it belongs to us. In the Greek the emphasis is on grace, *charis*, God graciously allows us to function in these supernatural gifts, available to the body, to any of us, at any time, or at least when specifically needed. In the 1970s, the emerging teaching focussed on you

---

[186] The New Testament gift of prophecy (as is our entire Christian existence) is likened to looking into a fuzzy mirror (1 Corinthians 13:12). First century mirrors did not have the clarity of our modern counterparts. Even so, prophecy is not to be despised but weighed (1 Thessalonians 5:20-21 & 1 Corinthians 14:29). Therefore, the possibility of being wrong or less than fully accurate is allowed for.

discovering your spiritual gift, it was very possessive in language. Misleading and unhelpful, for in a meeting you might have a 'prophet' and an 'interpreter of tongues', but without a 'healer' the group would be unable to pray for someone's healing – just ludicrous unbiblical nonsense!

Another interpretation given back then, from those not wanting to believe in the gifts, was that these gifts were God's instigated talents in a person's life. Therefore, a medic, a doctor or nurse had the 'gift of healing'. An overseas missionary with a flair for languages, the 'gift of tongues'. Again, nonsense!

The words Paul uses here in 1 Corinthians 12 are clear, *pneumatica* and *charismata*, these are supernatural spiritual manifestations of God's ministry[187], which are graciously given (therefore, available to any and all) as a *gift* (blessing) to the church.

The list in Ephesians 4, are described as gifts from Christ[188]. The context is directly linked to Jesus's resurrection victory and their purpose is for the ongoing equipping and maturing of the local

---

[187] The clarity, the gifts listed in 1 Corinthians 12:8-10 are all *supernatural* in essence, divinely given words of wisdom, words of knowledge, faith, healing, miraculous powers, prophecy, spiritual discernment, tongues and the interpretation of tongues.

The gift of tongues is described (1 Corinthians 13:1) as the *language of men*, as happened supernaturally in Acts 2:6, or *of angels*, perhaps the God-orientated and unintelligible words Paul describes in 1 Corinthians 14:2, 5, & 9.

Further explanations of the nine gifts listed in 1 Corinthians 12:8-10 can be found in my book, *School of Prophecy*.

[188] Ephesians 4:11, in the New Living Translation and Amplified Bible

church[189]. English translations of verse 11 vary, older *New International Versions* contained the word *some*, as does the *New American Standard Bible*, which is said to be one of the most accurate translations keeping to the original Greek.

> And He gave some as apostles, some as prophets,
> some as evangelists, some as pastors and teachers,
> **Ephesians 4:11 [NASB]**

The word *some* (which is clearly present in the Greek) has been dropped in modern translations. Perhaps when reading that only *some* are *evangelists*, gives too many believers a biblical excuse not to be a witness for Christ?

Scholars make two observations from this verse. The lack of the word *some* before the gift of teaching suggests that Paul was envisioning a joint role of a *pastor-teacher*. In many ways the history of the Protestant church seems to model such a belief. In my own theological training, there was a clear emphasis on teaching, less on pastoral studies, and pretty much zero content to equip me as an apostle, a prophet, or even an evangelist.

The second observation in interpreting the grammar of the original Greek, is to legitimately align the term *teacher* not only to the work of a pastor, but to all four of the gifts listed previously in the verse. Hence, the use of *some* becomes more logical. Christ

---

[189] Ephesians 4:12-13

has gifted His church with *some* Spirit-anointed teachers; some of these teach and equip us to be apostolic, some seek to nurture our prophetic gift, others train us in evangelism and finally some equip us in being pastoral. I liken this interpretation to being a pupil at a secondary school (aged 11-18), where everyone is taught mathematics and English, but not everyone is a Maths teacher or an English teacher. To summarise, the victorious and triumphant Christ has gifted His church with specific Spirit-anointed teachers, to equip the *entire* church in being apostolic, prophetic, evangelistic and pastoral. Again, in practice, gifted church leaders and gifted Bible teachers may operate in more than one of these areas. Returning to the school analogy, I sometimes had the same teacher for more than one subject.

Due to the context of these gifts, they are often referred to as the *equipping gifts*, or *ministry gifts*.

Let's turn to the list in our third passage, Romans 12:6-8. As stated earlier, the gifts in 1 Corinthians 12 are all supernatural, hence Paul's use of the word – *pneumatic*. In contrast, with the exception of prophecy, the list in Romans 12 are all akin to natural abilities. For example, teaching, leadership, encouragement, serving, showing mercy. Hence, some commentators refer to this grouping as *redemptive* or *motivational* gifts. Paul, before his Damascus Road experience was a gifted theologian and zealous in his faith[190]. After his conversion, he used his theological education to

---

[190] Philippians 3:5-6

educate the church and his spiritual zeal to establish churches in Asia Minor and Europe. It was as if God had redeemed his natural abilities to be used for the glory of God in expanding God's Kingdom. Likewise, some business minded people can be a true blessing in church leadership. I once heard a worship leader say, "When God converted me, He converted my guitar too." He already had an established musical career, but now he turned his skills and Spirit-anointed zeal to writing praise songs for the glory of God.

It makes sense. God can use your natural skills and talents for His glory. The flaw in this interpretation is the example of prophecy. Well, we just need to acknowledge the reality of the ancient world and its recognition of soothsayers. Not all psychics around today are charlatans, some of them truly believe they have 'a gift'. Weirdly I've met several such 'touched' people, whom prior to their Christian conversion were sensitive to auras and were occasionally predictive in their advice. Becoming a Christian a couple of these folk rejected their past as complete deceptions and alien to everything pure in God. Sadly, they also rejected the present-day reality of Holy Spirit gifts. A classic example of throwing the baby out with the bath water. The others, thankfully, found the ability to transfer their 'skill' to align with God's purposes, and started to move powerfully in *Christian* prophecy.

So, there you have it, a whirlwind tour of the spiritual gifts, gifts, and gifts.

- The *pneumatic gifts* to empower the church supernaturally in her ministry through signs and wonders[191].
- The *equipping gifts* to equip the entire church family.
- The *redemptive gifts* as God redeems previous skills and preferences and uses them for the glory of His Kingdom.

I believe there is merit in looking at these different types of gifts to help mature your personal discipleship and increase the effectiveness of your ability to minister to others.

The pneumatic gifts are graciously given as and when. Therefore, your ability to move in these gifts will simply require faith and compassion. Compassion, more than confidence, attracts the presence of God, and thus His anointing upon your life[192].

The equipping gifts, to teach and equip others in specific areas of ministry, will be linked to the fruitfulness of your spiritual ministry and natural skills. Remembering the school analogy, we're all called to be apostolic, prophetic, evangelistic and pastoral, but only *some* are gifted to teach these skills[193].

---

[191] Hebrews 2:4

[192] It was Christ's compassion that led to miracles, Matthew 14:14, 15:32 and 20:34. Without writing an essay, so very briefly, Jesus got baptised not for His sin (He had none!), but to identify with the brokenness of the world, therefore, due to His compassion, He immediately received a fresh Holy Spirit anointing as His public ministry began.

[193] "If that's the case, why aren't these four areas covered more explicitly in this discipleship book?" Good question. I don't personally see myself as a gifted evangelist or a significantly insightful pastor. The other gifts are referenced and expanded in the other books in this series.

GIFTS GIFTS GIFTS

The redemptive or motivational gifts are often discerned upon you by others in prayer, frequently affirming what you already know or are doing.

I've met many reluctant and inexperienced prophets keen to join the prayer ministry team because of their heart of mercy. And sadly the reverse, because prophetically inclined people operating without a pastoral heart can be a nightmare!

To be honest, any form of Christian ministry without a pastoral heart, without compassion is dangerous. As stated earlier, God's anointing is often attracted to our compassion.

Now then, with that truth ringing in our ears, linked to a clear emphasis on the relational nature of effective discipleship, we can now move to this book's appendices and unpack a number of practical aids to enhance our Christian maturity.

SCHOOL OF DISCIPLESHIP

APPENDIX A

Prayer Praise and Prophecy

Prayer has been described as the Christian's vital breath, and also as a mystery we all choose to embrace. Traditionally when we first think of prayer, our normal default setting, is presenting our petitions – asking God for stuff. Though we sort of know there's more to it than that, in practice old thinking often still prevails.

A Christian leader was facilitating their daytime evangelistic Bible study, which consisted of a mixed group of unchurched folk. He told the group that next week's topic was on prayer, adding, as an ad-lib, "Just out of interest, do any of you pray?" Almost every hand went up. He was amazed, and instinctively responded with a follow-up question, "About *what*?" They stared back equally amazed at his question.

"Well, what do you think? For our boyfriends to stay sober, our kids to stay in school, for money to feed the family and for the police and bailiffs to stay at bay. Why, what do you pray for?"

SCHOOL OF DISCIPLESHIP

He said he would answer that question next week. That experience gives us an intriguing insight into prayer that many regular church attendees may have been unaware of, nevertheless, it also serves to prove my earlier point – prayer is generally seen as asking for stuff.

Draw a big circle in your mind or on a piece of paper, if there's some to hand. Label that circle, 'prayer', for everything in that circle is prayer – all those needs and requests. Now draw a second circle within the first circle and label that 'praise'. That's right, genuine God-orientated praise *is* prayer. When we sing to God, honour God, and declare our love for Him – that's prayer.

Quick side note, religion can be described as the appearance of spiritual things but without the power or presence of God. Some traditional forms of liturgy have been spiritually and beautifully crafted to help convey our worship. However, these words can also be read from the page without any personal or divine connection. Therefore, I'm not saying when everyone sings a hymn they're praying, it all depends on the individual's heart and attitude. If our God-focussed language is a genuine reflection of our heart, then all praise is prayer.

Now draw a third circle, within the first circle and intersecting with the second circle. This is prophecy. If prophecy is simply sharing that which God has brought to mind, then prophecy is a form of prayer, because first you've had to listen and receive from God.

PRAYER PRAISE AND PROPHECY

Most personal prophecy operates in a 'prayer ministry' environment, where the discipline of faith-filled prayer is a given, and prophecy is expected. I take the connection between prayer and prophecy very seriously. In a prophetic activation session, I encourage the participants to first pray and bless the person they're going to prophesy over. From the overflow of the heart the mouth speaks[194], if you can't generously pray for your brother or sister in the Lord, then I doubt your prophetic utterance will be spiritually 'clean' and helpful in, strengthening, comforting and encouraging[195]. I teach the same to developing worship leaders, 'pray it, don't say it', nurture your spiritual language of prayer, and as a result, prophecy will flow as you develop the root of this discipline.

A final observation on corporate prayer, though I hope it's not too cynical. Within any Church small group most people are willing to share but far fewer are willing to pray out loud. Now before you rush to defend yourself and explain the differences of those two styles of communication, I accept – it is harder to pray out loud, for sure. Even so, let's not forget that prayer and corporate prayer are Christian disciplines, they need to be nurtured. They also need to be effectively modelled by others. Thankfully, amid some bad, boring and religious sounding examples in my youth, I also got exposed to some inspiring corporate prayer.

---

[194] Matthew 12:34b
[195] 1 Corinthians 14:3

SCHOOL OF DISCIPLESHIP

In April 1982, when I was only nineteen years old, I left sleepy Gloucestershire for a week of mission in Balham, south London. It changed my life! The full story is for a different time. Nevertheless, within those seven remarkable unforgettable days I experienced people praying simultaneous extempore prayers. Yes, that's right, they were all praying out loud at the same time their own prayers. Though our cerebral minds could dismiss it as somewhat out of order – just a noise. It wasn't, it was inspiring, encouraging, releasing, it allowed me to pray out loud with greater zeal and less fear. A significant stepping stone in my discipleship.

In 1988, at twenty-five, I was the pastor of a small rural Baptist Church. After one of my first morning services, and when we were both safely back home, my wife told me in no uncertain terms, *if I was ever going to pray in public again, I mustn't pray like that!* She added something along the lines, and I paraphrase from memory, *Pray from your heart not from your head. Stop overthinking your words, don't seek to be clever, seek to be genuine.* I loved her brave reprimand; it was one of the best things that ever happened to me to help and shape my public prayers.

A decade later we were in a different church in a very different location. A special early-January worship event had been called to launch the new year with God at the centre – it made sense. Quite a crowd gathered. The worship band set up and we all stood around, looking very much like an audience more than participating worshippers. I still vividly remember that night. It felt strange. The songs didn't really flow. They were the latest 'hits', yet it felt like we were going through the motions. Then, a friend of mine started to pray out loud; he was a retired Pentecostal minister forging a new career as a school administrator. I knew him, I knew something of his background, though I also knew many people just thought of him as the ageing bursar at some local fee-paying school. He prayed. The atmosphere changed. I felt it. Others clearly acknowledged it too. Unforgettable. It was like hearing Moses plead with God for His presence to come and manifest[196]. In fact, there wasn't much pleading, this man had authority in his voice and God responded. It was obvious this man had cultivated, over the years, a strong and confident prayer language with God.

Now here's a really important lesson for your discipleship. Most people in prayer meetings and church gatherings, etcetera, assume an almost passive position of being a spectator. On that cold January evening, that man pretty much touched an entire room with his zeal, and the worship that followed was far more intense and heartfelt. Most of us would be glad of the change in the spiritual atmosphere, allowing a better meeting to proceed. A true disciple would look on and *earnestly desire*[197] that gift of prayer. As I write these words, I'm reliving that event and recalling the times I've sought to follow that man's example. Not a copycat of his words or even demeanour, but to make sure when I enter a place of corporate worship, I carry the authority of God, I'm

---

[196] Exodus 33:15-18
[197] Purposely using the words of Paul from 1 Corinthians 14:1

focussed on being in step with the Spirit, and willing, as a sacrifice of praise, to be utterly vulnerable and honest in my God-infused language. Not a show! Not exuberant confidence, or the trait of an extrovert, but an honest Spirit-filled worshiper longing for God to fill the room with His *shekinah* glory[198].

Such expressed zeal doesn't always work. There are variables in corporate gatherings when we're seeking to flow in prayer, praise and prophecy. Our motives may not always be as clean as we would want them to be. The personal faith of others can have an enormous effect[199]. Time restrictions, tiredness, expectations, personal experiences, fears, doubts – the list is endless. But please, let's keep raising the bar, and expecting for more. We also need to learn to handle such disappointments with increased maturity, disciples need to learn, apply, reflect, learn again, adapt and develop, their personal spiritual maturity from every experience.

---

[198] The word, *shekinah* means 'dwelling' or 'He causes to dwell', in Hebrew it's used to describe specific manifestations of God's presence and glory. Such as God's presence in the burning bush of Exodus 3:2. The word doesn't appear in the Bible (like, Trinity), it came to be used during the intertestamental period by rabbis and scholars to explain many spiritual phenomena found in the Old Testament texts. Notably, the dedication of Solomon's Temple, when a 'cloud' of God's glory appeared and brought the proceedings to a halt (1 Kings 8:10-11). In addition, the Hebrew for *glory* comes from the word *weight*. In English we often attach this word giving us the phrase, *the weight of His glory*. To this day, in times of intensive corporate praise, the weight of His glory can be tangible and people either choose to kneel, or lie prostrate, others just fall over under the weight of the *shekinah* glory.

[199] Mark 6:5, even Jesus faced restrictions in His ministry due to the lack of faith of others

PRAYER PRAISE AND PROPHECY

The place of praise

Imagine a prayer meeting. Our experiences and expectations of a church prayer meeting will vary enormously. So, from your own thoughts, where does praise fit in? A couple of songs at the beginning? Perhaps only a couple, after all we've come to pray. What a nonsense that statement is. Praise *is* prayer! A visiting Bible teacher at a conference once said. "If you only have 10 minutes to pray, then praise God for eight of them, it's surprising after that how much you can fit into two minutes." The context for his comment was personal prayer, but could you imagine the indignation that would manifest from some of our congregants if the church prayer meeting was 80% praise.

> ... angels joined in bearing gifts. Individuals, one after the other, had quite extraordinary power encounters with the manifest presence of God as He seemed to have brought angels to us to affirm and equip different people.

From years of experience the best prayer meetings I've attended have all been dominated with praise and waiting on God. When I say *best*, I mean fruitful, powerful, spiritually dynamic. Though some of these things won't be known until afterwards or weeks later. Though one memorable occasion, angels joined in bearing gifts. Individuals, one after the other, had quite extraordinary power encounters with the manifest presence of God as He seemed to have brought angels to us to affirm and equip different people. It was marvellous beyond words, and unavoidably humorous too. Most of the people in attendance were middle-aged and some considerably older. As different individuals were touched by God their bodies manifested in ways that I (and others) thought could be detrimental to their health. I remember constantly repositioning cushions around a woman of ninety to avoid her having a serious accident. We wept, we laughed – it was glorious. Oh, and yes there was lasting fruit, a new city-wide prayer initiative, and a sudden change in our ability to discern and become more authoritative in our intercession[200].

One last story. Once, in a fairly traditional church prayer meeting a quite elderly woman started to pray out loud. Her language was full of praise, she loved God and the evidence of her personal devotional life overflowed into her prayer. Then the language turned to society. Clearly, she felt the world was a difficult and hostile place, in this change of focus she still praised God, declaring His Lordship over various institutions and work environments. Was this intercession? She wasn't asking for anything specific, but generally wanting God's Kingdom to come.

---

[200] We transitioned from pleading petitions to clearer declarations due to increased discernment. We were learning about the mystery of prayer, and God seemed to allow us clearer access to the heavenly realms. Some of the skills were transferrable, though some of the anointed authority was only for those particular situations.

PRAYER PRAISE AND PROPHECY

Whatever it was in terms of prayer – it was biblical![201] Now the language changed again, though the flow of her language was unhindered, she never seemed to pause for breath. The focus had become even more specific, a meeting requiring God's favour, a school teacher needing courage, a business manager needing wisdom. Did she know these people? The language was subtle, even so, she was praying as if she knew of these forthcoming events. Was she prophesying? I'll never forget that morning. She prayed from an overflowing heart, praise, thanksgiving, petitions, intercessions, declarations and prophetic utterances. It was all there. Witnessing it was better than attending any seminar on the subject or reading a chapter in a book. Prayer, praise and prophecy flowing from a lover's heart who clearly knew God personally. There ends the lesson.

---

[201] Matthew 6:10

APPENDIX B

Read the Bible

The evangelistic tract I read shortly after my dream encounter with Jesus ended with three statements, pray every day, read the Bible every day, and find a church to attend. It wasn't much to go on. Hopefully we can offer a little more advice these days, especially as we discover that many Christians struggle in one, if not in all of these areas[202].

Throughout my formal schooling I had a below average reading age, I struggled to spell and had little motivation to read books. So as a new believer, aged thirteen, the Bible and the need to read

---

[202] In this appendix we'll be looking at fresh approaches to Bible reading, and in the next chapter, I'll unpack more engaging ways to pray. I haven't got a chapter on church. It's such a broad subject with many variables. The sixteenth century Anabaptists said, a congregation needs to be both *inviting* and *invitational*. A place where you feel welcomed, and a place you would be happy to bring others to. Here's some other possible questions. Is the Spirit being honoured? Is the Bible being taught? Is leadership equipping and releasing, or controlling and restricting? Are there new people and new believers? Are you being valued or lost in the crowd? Can you be a participant or just a spectator?

READ THE BIBLE

it was a daunting task. A youth Bible study even more so, as the leaders would insist on reading the Bible passage round the group out loud, with each person present taking one verse. This did not aid my comprehension, I just frantically counted ahead and checked out the words in my appointed section. Curse the guy who accidentally read two verses! I'm just saying, it was a cold sweat nightmare scenario – please note all you budding church youth workers.

When it came to prayer, my only knowledge was from my school experience. Yes, that's right, we still prayed in school back then. So, prayer was something you did in a school assembly, with your eyes closed and your hands together. Read one of my other **School of** books to discover how I eventually prayed a prayer of salvation with my eyes tightly shut in the privacy of my own bedroom, having painstakingly memorised the words of the classic salvation prayer, line by line – I didn't know any better, well at least it worked.

Finally, church, to me was nothing more than that odd looking old building at the corner of a street. I knew nothing about evangelicals, or non-conformists, liberal teaching and nominal believers. So having been a Christian for less than two weeks, I got up the courage to attend the local gothic styled church building. Let's just say it was an experience I never want to repeat! Yet, somehow, this new disciple made it through. God is faithful and a Good Shepherd; and my decision back in July 1976 to follow Christ proved to be genuine. God found me as an ignorant and flawed teenager, yet within that ignorance, His grace, love and friendship[203] leaked into my life. Thank you, Jesus.

Almost a year earlier the visiting Gideons[204] had given every pupil in my school one of their New Testaments. It was now the Summer, I'd managed to successfully recite a prayer with my eyes shut and my hands together, then over the next three months I pretty much read that New Testament from cover to cover. To be honest, with my background, I felt that was a small miracle in and of itself, though in all honesty my *understanding* of what I was reading was minimal.

At this time, I also had got my hands on a copy of Malcolm and Alwyn's 1974 album, *Wildwall,* I listened to it endlessly. These Christian folk-rock songs acted as my *School of Discipleship.* Perhaps that's how I discovered and nurtured a far more relaxed and non-religious form of Christianity. My faith was emerging as relational, even intimate; Jesus was someone I loved – that reality changes your prayer life, it really does. Once I had discovered you didn't need to observe a particular posture when praying, I became far more relaxed. Even your approach to handling the Bible changes with your increased ideas of God's accessibility and approachability.

---

[203] 2 Corinthians 13:14
[204] The same international organisation that get Bibles placed in almost every hotel room around the world.

READ THE BIBLE

There's an old Vineyard Music song that closes with these three repeated phrases,

> *I need You,*
> *I want You,*
> *I love Your presence.*[205]

That's a great revelatory progression. The reality of God, quite logically, is a *need* we all have. We simply need God. We were designed to fellowship with God. But do we *want* God? Outside of a particular need, is He our go-to choice? Do I *want* to fellowship with other believers? Do I *want* to read my Bible? Somehow, I had to transition from the instruction that implied my *need* to read the Bible, to the relational choice of *wanting* to read the Bible. This change in motivation is significant. I once heard a seasoned pastor use the phrase, *start in the flesh and move to the spirit*. It seemed way dodgy at the time, but in reality, it works. Later I'll explain the journey from a *decision* to a *delight*.

At the close of John chapter 6, after 5000 people are miraculously fed, they all decide to walk away from Jesus, He turns, to the Twelve asking if they want to go too. Simon Peter admits, having been with Jesus this long, hearing His life-changing words, "Where could I go?" (John 6:68), he chooses to stay. Fast forward to the end of that same Gospel and Peter is declaring his love for

---

[205]*Come and Fill Me Up*, Copyright © 1997 Brian Doerksen, Mercy/Vineyard Publishing. All rights reserved.

Jesus[206]. Later the apostle John captures the circular instruction to love through obedience, for Jesus commanded us to walk in love.[207]. God is not desiring obedience out of fear, but out of the motivation of love.

Throughout my ministry I've used a progressive teaching tool to express the *love-obedience* notion in Christian discipleship.

- Decision
- Discipline
- Delight

Everything we do requires a decision. The decision to choose to engage with God's Holy Bible, that's your choice. Then we need some form of discipline to keep us faithful to our decision. Perhaps setting the alarm clock earlier, swapping a TV programme for your Bible time – I did that for a highly productive season. However, discipline is generally always required to achieve a task you wouldn't naturally complete. Within the truth of that, you can either live your Christian life safeguarded with disciplines, or you can develop a genuine relationship with God to where a discipline becomes a delight. I love the feeling of driving home, imagining when I get into my house, I'll put the kettle on prepare myself a generous mug of tea and sit down with my Bible. But of course,

---

[206] John 21:15-17
[207] 2 John 1:6, love is a command, and obedience to that command leads to love.

it's not *just* my Bible; I'm actually going to be hanging out with God with *our* favourite book!

I love this verse,

> Jesus did many other things as well. If every one of them were written down, I suppose that even the whole world would not have room for the books that would be written.
> **John 21:25**

I believe in divine inspiration and supreme authority of the Old and New Testament Scriptures, which are the written Words of God – fully trustworthy for faith and conduct. Wow! That last sentence could almost be found in some form of *statement of faith*. In addition, I'm also aware that this verse, John 21:25, isn't to be taken literally but is a form of hyperbole (deliberate exaggeration) to make a point. The point? Jesus did loads of things and John's Gospel barely captures the tip of the iceberg.

John's Gospel has a very different feel compared to the Synoptics, which focus on His Galilean ministry, whereas John has far more of a Jerusalem focus. It could be argued John's Christology is more developed than the earlier Gospels. But before I launch off and write extensively on this, all four documents *also* have much in common. Therefore, John's hyperbole becomes of greater interest. Imagine, amid so much possible material, we only have four quite limited and focussed Gospels for the church to learn about our Saviour. My conclusion is simple, what we have is of great significance and perhaps one of the most significant passages has to be the feeding of the five thousand, as it is the only miracle (apart from the resurrection) that appears in all four Gospels. That must be important, what do you think?

Now, take John's hyperbole about Jesus and apply it to the entire workings of God. If Christ's recorded ministry of just three years would require a library the size of the planet, then how much more space would we need to store the *Complete Works of Yahweh*?

So now, suddenly the sixty-six books in the Bible are just a drop in the ocean. It may well be hard to grasp the full significance of the books we have, when they contain so many lists, Jesus's own genealogy (twice!), what of the opening chapters of 1 Chronicles? In Ezra, we discover that someone has been counting livestock and this inventory gets included in God's inspired Scriptures. This is *not* an argument against the authority of Scripture, I'm building my case for its total and absolute significance – if only we can grasp the mind of God in telling us such details.

I have developed a simple and memorable threefold approach to engaging with the Bible, I call it, *CSI*. Not crime scene investigators, though in a sense, that is our task, to look at the evidence of the words and discern their eternal relevance.

READ THE BIBLE

CSI

1. **Content** – not necessarily the broader context, just the actual content. What did you read? I love the look on people's faces, when we've read a Bible passage and I immediately tell them to close their Bibles – shock, surprise. But then I ask, "So what was happening in that passage?" Some of the answers are easy. Though it's always interesting to note what's remembered and what may have been forgotten or overlooked. We can't presume we all heard the same thing. C is for Content!

2. **Significance** – when it would need the planet (some exaggeration) to house the contents of Christ's initial three-year ministry, then what's the significance of God authorizing these words for the Bible? What's so important (significant) about this passage? At times, that can be a tough question to answer.

   I have a theory, just a theory, just my own personal theory and it goes like this. God designed the Bible as an amazing resource to aid our interaction with Him. It requires His presence to have true value. It's like some electrical appliance, that requires to be plugged into a power source. Likewise, God's involvement is needed for us to find significant spiritual interpretation. The book is Spirit inspired[208], that's like telling us which original language it was written in. If a book is in

---
[208] 2 Timothy 3:16

SCHOOL OF DISCIPLESHIP

French, you need to know French to read it and understand it. The Bible is written in 'Holy Spirit Inspiration' – that's the original language, before Hebrew or Chaldean or Aramaic or Greek lectionaries helped form the words onto the page, God spoke through His Spirit, and we need to operate in that language to find the right interpretation. Hence the focus on *keeping in step* in the first half of this book.

There's more to my humble theory. There are bits in the Bible that are easy to understand. The language isn't ambiguous, and the instructions are still clear thousands of years later. There are also bits that aren't so clear. In my theory, that's done deliberately by God, so that we need God's real-time presence to aid our understanding. It's truly wonderful, because we have an ancient book, yet the author is still alive! The Bible has easy bits, less easy bits, harder stuff, and some downright difficult and obscure imagery. I truly believe that's all part of God's plan, as it seeks to stop us simply becoming skilled archivists or theoretical classicists – we need *Him* to enlighten our minds! Perhaps we get a glimpse of *Jehovah Sneaky* in this verse?

> It is the glory of God to conceal a matter;
>   to search out a matter is the glory of kings.
> **Proverbs 25:2**

READ THE BIBLE

Revelation 1:5b says that we have become kings and priests, so one of our is to discover the wonders of God[209].

3. **Implication** – if God's words are Spirit-breathed and have value to teach, correct and train us in all righteousness[210], then, what are the implications of *these* verses? The weakest area in most midweek Bible studies and even in some pulpits is the application. Perhaps, in our UK culture, we don't want to be overly prescriptive. I'd argue that discipleship demands an application, otherwise it's not discipleship, just information. So finally, **CSI** ends with the tough question,

"After assessing the content, and unearthing its significance – so what? What's the implication of these verses?"

In a Bible study group, we can sometimes over complicate the Bible with too much context, the historical setting, the passage's textual genre, or even the etymology of some of the original words. These things can be helpful, but such tools and knowledge need to be used wisely. For example, if explaining to someone for the very first time what a hamburger is, the use of etymology to understand the root of the word, will only lead you to discover it's a food substance originating from Hamburg, in Germany. As your out-of-town visitor sits there with the menu trying to order lunch – they are none the wiser!

---

[209] Isaiah 45:3
[210] 2 Timothy 3:16-17

SCHOOL OF DISCIPLESHIP

The *CSI* approach to a weekly church-based Bible study should work in most settings. Another simple (though not necessarily easy) approach are the set questions that govern the *Discovery Bible Study*[211]. These questions were first designed for evangelistic and early discipleship purposes. But as few of us were ever truly and deliberately discipled, they're still highly effective. From years of experience and observations, often it's the questions in a small group Bible study that lead to frustration, tangents and the general inefficiency of such a study to be an act of effective discipleship. A badly crafted question can often carry a hidden agenda. The group leader may have some unhelpful bias to emphasise. There's an alternative and simple solution, here are the four *DBS* questions you can ask at pretty much *every* Bible study.

- What does this passage say about God?
- What does this passage say about humanity?
- What is this passage saying to *you*?
- Who else needs to hear these truths?

Note that the third question is deliberately personal, and that the fourth question is either unashamedly evangelistic, or at least gives the participant the opportunity to stretch their faith pastorally in the coming days. Originally designed to be applied to the seven miracle passages in John's Gospel, I've known small

---

[211] DBS has its own website, but it's hard to detect its origins or whether the abbreviation or concept is under any official copyright.

groups use the same questions them with a variety of Scriptures. You can even use them personally in your devotions. If the passage clearly doesn't seem to offer an answer to one of the questions, move on, but first take your time, think outside of box and ask God for His ideas – get relational with the God who desires to fellowship with you. My little Bible analysis theory is based on the premise that God always wants to be involved in your Bible reading. Some people say you ought to pray before reading the Bible or pray after you've read the passage. Rubbish! I say, talk to God while you're reading.

Also – when at all possible, read the Bible *out loud*. It truly helps your mind to engage with the words, and your heart to sense the emotions within the passage. I've heard so many testimonies of the tangible presence of God entering rooms as people read (almost desperately) out loud, desiring a fresh connection with God. One of the main flaws of our prayer life, is simply that, they're *our* prayers, *our* language, *our* messed-up emotions and bias ideas. Sometimes we need to shut up, stop over-thinking in ever decreasing circles, and read *His* words! Loudly, to fill the environment and change the spiritual and emotional atmosphere. Remember, the most powerful prayers begin with praying Scripture. Let God's language, God's truths, God's bias, God's values, fill your mouth, your soul and spirit. Make the decision and find the discipline to read the Bible out loud for ten minutes every day. Within two weeks your life will be stronger in God – absolute truth. Prove me wrong if you can. Take *'the Psalm 34 challenge'*, as mentioned earlier in this book. Read this psalm out loud, twice

SCHOOL OF DISCIPLESHIP

through daily, for at least three days. Your spiritual life will change! And this will become a regular delight, with other passages, in your walk with God.

Read the Bible! What more can I say?

What about using daily notes, a phone app, or a reading schedule for the year? All helpful, though I've personally never connected that way, too much schoolroom culture and a feeling of doing a daily chore. I'm committed to keeping it relational, prayerful and Spirit-led; though let's not fool ourselves, we still need discipline during tougher times. Decision, discipline and delight is a spectrum we wander along (back and forth) in the different seasons of our life.

The beauty of Spirit-inspired Scripture is that when you really don't want to read, yet you muster the energy to reluctantly read, those few choice verses can instantly disperse the clouds and bring a perceived distant God closer than a friend. I've experienced this time and time again. I cling to Christ's first response to a nagging devil, *'We shall not live by bread alone, but by every word that comes from the mouth of God*[212].*'*

---

[212] Matthew 4:4

READ THE BIBLE

Don't treat the Bible like a textbook – it's alive and active[213]. The words on the page don't change, but when you open it up the breath of God is fresh and inviting.

---
[213] Hebrews 4:12

Appendix C

Time With God

The classic 'quiet time' is not everyone's cup to tea. Many Christians come to faith in their youth, and failure to spend time every day with God, reading their Bibles and praying, can often lead to feelings of guilt. Unfortunately, their struggles can't always be easily resolved by their older and wiser congregants, as they too have often ongoing difficulties with their own personal devotions.

The first step in finding a workable solution is to re-emphasise the relational nature of our walk with God. Personal devotions cannot be reduced to a reading schedule or a quick glance at some daily devotional notes. Nor can it be completely restricted to a set 'God time' that may carry inadvertently a perceived divide between your spiritual life and the rest of your daily activities. Though that sounds a bit extreme, the spiritual-secular divide still exists. In some church cultures, it's often unnecessarily reenforced between acknowledging the difference between ordained ministers and the laity. It's also present quite dangerously in the world of work. If you consider your non-church-based job as a secular job, then it's going to be much harder for you to see yourself as an apostle or prophet in that environment. In the past I've known churches 'ordain' some of their health workers and IT staff, to remove the unnecessary divide between God's work (narrowly understood as that of the church and missionaries), as opposed to the vast majority of people who can be a witness and even a strategic influencer across a breadth of occupations. God's work doesn't start on a Sunday morning, it starts in the office, the classroom and indeed, the moment you wake in your house. Technically, even before that, as an Argentine pastor once led a seminar entitled, *Stop Sleeping with the Enemy*, an insightful message about how to lie down in peace and reclaim your sleep for God's glory. Anyway, I digress.

Effective *Time with God* needs two ongoing spiritual disciplines,

1. Direct Focus – time set aside specifically to be with God.
2. General Awareness – engaging with God in the everyday.

Direct focus

Following Jesus's instructions in Matthew 6, we are to pray by finding a quiet place, where we can close the door and be with our Father in secret. Not secret in some clandestine way, but in private, a place where we grow in God free from distractions. Did you know that a church wedding in the UK is a public affair? Though we invite our own guests, a photographer to capture the moment, in British law, the doors to a church building, during a wedding ceremony, cannot be locked. Contrast this with the honeymoon! Intimacy needs privacy. Jesus models this again, by waking early in the morning and stealing away to be with His Father before the events of the day demand His public presence[214].

Traditionally, evangelical Christians have called these sessions, the *quiet time*. Many of us were told early on in our discipleship to read the Bible and pray every day. Some of us, may have been helped in these instructions. Such as pray before reading the Bible or keep a prayer journal and jot down your prayer requests so you can tick them off when answered. Often these instructions carry the default bias that Bible reading is about study and that prayers are petitionary. Hopefully if you've read this book from the beginning, you'll know I disagree with both those notions. Our relational approach to God may not completely change the agenda of our devotions, but the cultural change, of learning to

---
[214] Mark 1:35

hang out with God, should reset the traditional boundaries around prayer, study, meditation and praise.

Direct focus is deliberate time with God. We ought to come to this discipline in the context of worship rather than study. Again, like so much Westernised Christianity, 'school room' thinking can too easily eclipse the joy of knowing God. The living words of God are reduced to a difficult textbook, and prayer is far more about us talking to God, then listening to what the Spirit might be saying.

I make no apology for using the phrase, *hanging out with God*. Though to make it sound more biblical, I could say, *fellowshipping with the Holy Spirit*.

In Revelation 3:20, we find Jesus knocking on the door of our heart with a dinner invitation! That's relational!

Don't forget the focus we had in Chapter 1, God is *relational and revelatory*. Therefore, time spent with Him ought to be relaxed and enlightening. Well, perhaps not all the time. In reality, we get tired, distracted, and presumptuous about His words. I think my first instruction in having a *quiet time*, included that once I'd read the set Bible passage (generally the minimum of a chapter a day), I needed to ask the questions, Who? When? What? Why? It sounded like my school's English Language comprehension tests. I hope my alternative approach of **CSI**, in the last chapter was more appealing.

SCHOOL OF DISCIPLESHIP

We can't afford to allow time with God to become a chore or an inconvenience amid a busy schedule.

I've often experienced the testimony proclaimed in Psalm 122.

> I rejoiced with those who said to me,
>   'Let us go to the house of the LORD.'
> **Psalm 122:1**

Whenever I made the decision to fellowship with others, or just to simply sit down with God – I've never regretted it.

Let's now look at how to nurture a time of *direct focus,* without getting bored.

The 3-minute+ quiet time

Here's a structure to get you going. The focus is on prayer, because the essential foundation for healthy discipleship is on our relationship with God.

So, using Jesus's own template, think of the Lord's Prayer broken down into 8-points, with its corporate language re-written in the first person for you[215].

---

[215] In a previous book I suggested the plural language of the Lord's Prayer may not have been because Jesus was teaching a group of people, but intentional to keep our prayers, cultural for the time, at a community level rather than make our time with God heavily individualist. I still think, asking for 'our daily bread' as a church community, or a location, or even as a country has value, as would our ability to acknowledge corporate sin and forgive others at a community level. Nevertheless, for this exercise, in this immediate context, we'll go old school.

TIME WITH GOD

1. My Father
2. Hallowed be Your name
3. Your Kingdom come, Your will be done
4. On Earth as it is in heaven
5. Provide for my daily needs
6. Forgive me my sins, as I forgive those who sin against me
7. Lead me,
8. Not into temptation but deliver me from evil.

The 8-fold focus is quite self-explanatory. As you begin to pray, use the four fingers on each hand to lead you through the points – then end triumphantly with a double thumbs up as you announce with joy and victory,

Yours is the Kingdom, the power and the glory – Amen!

Childish? Actions attached to words are a proven teaching aid. In recent months I've taken to riding the bus rather than driving the car, and I do this on my seat. Not out loud, but I do use my fingers to help me through each section. Especially if I over ad-lib, they help me not to lose my place.

Here's the prayer again, with some explanation in case it's needed.

1. The invite to address God as, Father. Even though He resides in heaven, the language is both awe inspiring, yet intimate and relational.

SCHOOL OF DISCIPLESHIP

2. The decision, by you, to honour His name, in your words, actions and thoughts. In all things, respect and honour God's call on your life. Including the presence of the Holy Spirit, residing within you. That's quite a commitment, and for some of you – quite a challenge.
3. Before we bring any of our own requests, our calling is to seek first His Kingdom and righteousness[216]. Your desire to prioritise God's Kingdom, is an invitation to God to pilot your life and decisions.
4. On Earth as in heaven, or in other words – right here, right now. Our prayer is to see the evidence of His advancing Kingdom in the environments where we function. His outstretched hand bringing salvation, healing and deliverance. You might have situations in mind, people, loved ones, difficult problems. Learn to pray into these things God's will and Kingdom language, rather than your own hoped-for solutions.
5. Note that before we've even asked for our daily needs, we've already covered a lot of ground as we align our heart and desires with God's Kingdom and will. Now, we pray, not for wants, but for our presenting needs.
6. The importance of keeping short accounts with God, not allowing things to get out of control. Confess to your loving Father your mistakes, asking for His gracious forgiveness. Then, without hesitation, do the same for others, releasing forgiveness to any who have deliberately, or thoughtlessly,

---

[216] Matthew 6:33

or even unknowingly, caused you pain. Forgiving others is not about excusing the guilty, but more about removing the pain and bitterness from your own heart. Unforgiveness is like drinking poison hoping the other person will drop dead! Forgiving people their debts, is literally handing over your spiritual creditors into God's hands. Selling the bad debt and leaving it in God's court. Therefore, forgiveness is in order to keep your heart pure and free from the pain of emotional damage, and time consumed harbouring vengeful thoughts.

The important thing is to receive God's forgiveness, that restores you to worship in spirit and in truth, and to forgive others so bitterness or resentment can't take root in your soul.

7. Lead me – I'm sure God doesn't deliberately lead us into temptation. So, a strategic comma placed here, stresses our desire for His leadership over our life.
8. Trusting that such divine leadership will keep us from temptation and the subtle schemes of the enemy.
9. & 10. *Bam! Bam!* All for His Kingdom, His power and His glory! Amen and amen.

To engage with all that content at a personal level with an element of reflection and your own bespoke prayers – that's going to take you at least 3-minutes, if not much longer. It all depends on how thoughtful you become over each statement. Avoid treating the original words with either a sense of over-familiarity or untouchable liturgy. Jesus gave us these pointers, beginning with the invite to commune with His Father – *our* Father, *your* Father. Keep it relational, and the two of you will have a precious and long overdue good natter together. Oh yeah, create some space around the different statements, in case He wants to interrupt, and perhaps remind you of something or someone.

My personal devotions have gone through a number of regenerations. I've used liturgy, especially the words created by our Celtic Christian forefathers and mothers. As a worship leader, I've used Scripture in song, combining praise and extempore declarations. For certain seasons, often instigated by the Spirit, I've separated my Bible reading time from my prayer focus. Then using simple prayer mnemonics I've cultivated longer times of focussed prayer.

PRAY
      P – praise
      R – review (the past 24 hours) or r for repent, or both!
      A – ask
      Y – yield, surrender afresh to God's will and align yourself with His Kingdom.

ACTS
      A – adoration
      C – confession
      T – thanksgiving
      S – supplication (that's the asking bit)

I normally use these mnemonics with a notebook. This is not a traditional prayer journal, where you might record your requests and insightful thoughts. This is the discipline of using pen and paper to physically write, scribble, circle, underline, and repeat my spoken prayers. This is probably one of the *best* disciplines I've used to add focus to the content of my prayers.

It's not simply about recording your prayers, but the real-time discipline of 'emotionally' writing out what you're seeking to say. In education, physical writing, not typing or recording an audio, has proven to help students to better understand and remember their recorded notes. I know it's the gadget laden and digitally connected twenty-first century, but thankfully, we're still able to buy a pen and a notebook. It's worth it – believe me.

By the way, my handwriting is atrocious. That's not the point, I'm not creating a journal to look back on, but simply the actual scribbled words, legible or not, that form my prayers, cries and yearnings.

Where does the Bible fit in?

First, read simple and accessible passages; Mark's Gospel, James, Philippians and 1 Thessalonians. Then read them again, why not? You're bound to discover new things, and God will never grow tired of reviewing some of His all-time classics with you.

SCHOOL OF DISCIPLESHIP

Second, like we did with the Lord's Prayer – pray Scripture. The Bible is full of prayers, songs and potential prayers. So, they're a great place to develop your prayer language.

Here's a quick starter for five,

1. Ephesians 3:14-21, discover Christ's four-dimensional love and so much more!
2. Psalms 23, for you, for life, for every situation.
3. Revelation 4, my second home, learn to rest, worship, and be exhilarated in the celestial courts.
4. Psalm 1, be blessed and recalibrated into God's ways.
5. 2 Timothy 1:3-14, discover Paul's heart, sharing and praying specifically for Timothy, but there's plenty here we can all pull on.

So, there you have it, *Direct Focus*, some starter tips to avoid the obvious and the often-ineffective ways to spend time with God.

Learn to pray,

- use the language of Jesus
- use mnemonics
- use a notepad and pen to focus your language
- use Scripture – by developing your own key life-impacting verses.

Whatever you choose to do – don't be boring!

TIME WITH GOD

General awareness

This discipline helps to connect our everyday activities with God. I first encountered this practice as a young believer at school in answer to the question, "How do we avoid forgetting about God through a busy day?" The answer was simple, attach a short prayer to a repeated daily task. For school, it was the need to open, and hold open for staff, the multiple pairs of fire doors that broke up our school corridors into fire safe and protected areas. Though the majority of our school time was in a classroom, as we moved from class to class, the constant need to open a door was unavoidable. Simple. Even easy. Open a door and speak briefly to God. This Christian life-hack is quite the game-changer. After leaving school, I soon developed other areas where I could nurture spontaneous prayer. I've used the following for decades,

1. Putting the kettle on. A very British past-time.
2. Walking upstairs. This only works if you live in a house with more than one floor. Sometimes this moment of prayer became so distracting, I'd forget why I was going upstairs in the first place.
3. Walking away from my parked car. Perhaps this started when attending a church in a rough part of London, and I quite naturally prayed that the car would still be there on my return. It soon developed into a regular prayer opportunity, every time I found myself walking away from my parked car. Ask yourself, if you're on your own, what do you think

about when locking your bike, leaving your car or riding a bus? It's an opportunity to chat with God.

General awareness is a simply instilled discipline, you set the boundaries and frequency, whatever it takes to keep God's presence fresh within your daily routines.

In this digital age, I've heard of people setting their smart watches to vibrate every 50 minutes, to encourage a regular life of praise and thanksgiving. I know this, because on one occasion I witnessed the conference speaker's moment of surprise and sudden change of language when their watch went off during their teaching session.

The simplicity and almost childlike approaches to invest in a prayer life triggered by *general awareness*, has great value and reward. Keeping God in the everyday helps significantly in keeping in step with His Spirit.

In addition to these deliberate prayer *triggers,* the discipline of *general awareness* starts to become a way of life. I often misread posters, replacing the actual words with something perhaps more spiritual. Even road sign declaring a street, *One Way,* makes me smile, remembering a Larry Norman song of the same title that speaks of the exclusivity of Christ's work for salvation. *General awareness* makes you observant and prayerful as you walk around, perhaps interpreting the clutter around a person's home as a physical manifestation of a troubled and cluttered life. A group of us back in 1992 were prayer-walking a seriously neglected suburb of London. Some of us noticed the strap line of the local green grocers', *Where Only the Best Will Do.* We felt it was a word from God. Within three months we'd planted a church, desiring excellence in all we did, within a year we baptised our first converts, and a year later appointed a part-time pastor.

Jesus reacted to and interpreted the things around Him, once He observed a fig tree without fruit. I'm not saying we should curse things[217], but becoming increasingly spiritually observant will develop the integrity of our discipleship.

Integrity? How come?

Being a follower of Jesus is not a hobby. It must never be reduced to a single compartment within our busy life. It's not a religion, requiring weekly observation to some form of ceremony or ritual.

Christianity is a relationship the Living God, Yahweh. The Creator God of Genesis 1, the covenant God of Abraham, Isaac and Jacob. The God of rescue, the God of Moses, and of all His peoples and even aliens who align themselves to His purposes, such as Rahab and Ruth. The God, who was there before there was a before, and

---

[217] Mark 11:12-25, this fig-tree narrative encircles the event of Jesus clearing the Temple, it's all about the dangers of appearance over substance. It serves a particular teaching purpose. Please note, I am using it as a *descriptive* example of attaching spiritual truths to the everyday, not as a *prescriptive* endorsement to criticise all evidence of religiosity.

the God who came in person – Jesus. The God of the Twelve, Paul, Barnabas and others. The God who knows you better than you know yourself. The God of yesterday, today and forever the same, who was, and is and is to come. Like the most extraordinary piece of hi-tech wireless equipment, when in your heart you speak His name (no matter the language) you have instant personal access to Him – the Everlasting Unchanging Creator God of the Bible. Can I hear an Amen? Or simply a mind blown – *Wow!*

That's my God. Do you know Him?

Answering that last question in the positive, combined with an eager desire to know more of Him, is probably one of the best definitions of discipleship.

Appendix D

Solitude Simplicity and Submission

Much of our discipleship is a matter of making choices. Therefore, this section is an appendix rather than a chapter, to create an element of choice rather than simply drown you in more words. Making healthy personal choices empowers us and starts to activate the true and powerful freedom we have in Christ[218].

Freedom is a precious thing. Wars are fought for it. Lives are sacrificed for it, and it's at the heart of Christ's redemptive work.

> It was for freedom that Christ has set us free.
> **Galatians 5:1**

---

[218] Galatians 5:1

SCHOOL OF DISCIPLESHIP

Richard Foster wrote a classic Christian book, *Celebration of Discipline* – and it's still in print. It's an exhaustive volume covering twelve Christian discipline, such as meditation, prayer, worship, fasting and celebration. A number of these disciplines appear in my own books, so for now, I'll focus on a simple threefold alliteration.

- solitude
- simplicity
- submission

These things may not come easy to you, or even seem attractive, nevertheless, their real value, if you choose freely to engage with them, will help your discipleship grow exponentially.

In the parable of the farmer sowing seeds, many seeds came to nothing, stolen by the birds for food, dying in shallow ground or strangled through lack of adequate weeding. The successful seeds multiplied, thirty times, sixth times, even one hundred times[219]. Such is the obvious manifesting difference between Christians that barely cope and those that have learnt to be more than conquerors[220].

---

[219] Matthew 13:1-23
[220] Romans 8:37

SOLITUDE SIMPLICITY AND SUBMISSION

Solitude

Biblical examples could be Jesus rising early in the morning to steal away and get some precious one-on-one time with His Father[221]. Add to this daily discipline, the 40 days in the wilderness, having been filled with the Spirit, Jesus is led by the Spirit and as a result returns empowered by the Spirit[222]. This was a significant one-off event in preparation for His earthly ministry. Though this episode is remembered mainly for the temptations Jesus faced, these tactics from the enemy actually backfired. Satan sought to question Jesus's identity and offer Him some shortcuts to reaching similar, though seriously alternative, goals. Thinking Jesus was vulnerable after His 40-day ordeal, Satan completely underestimated God and His Kingdom values. After 40 days of fasting during a Spirit-inspired period of solitude, Christ was probably never stronger!

Paul seems to have had a similar equipping experience, when he references his time in the desert after his conversation, which shaped his theology and fellowship with God[223]. Later we encounter John and his enforced solitude from the norm, as he is exiled onto the island of Patmos, the result being the extraordinary Book of Revelation[224]. True, it's not everyone's cup of tea, and still not easy to fathom, but undoubtedly it contains

---

[221] Mark 1:35
[222] Luke 4:1 & 14
[223] Galatians 1:11-12, 17-18.
[224] Revelation 1:9-10

stunning revelations of Jesus, glorified and victorious and still ministering His work of salvation.

Elijah twice found himself alone. One clearly God instigated[225]. The second, during a bout of depression and self-doubt, is graciously redeemed and used powerfully, extended by God to inaugurate fresh purpose and revelations[226].

Timeout is important. But not simply to be alone, but to be productive with God. Again, we seek to avoid formulas which subtly place us in the driving seat, I've experienced so-called 'retreat days' that have left little space for God and left me more puzzled and exhausted than refreshed and inspired. We need to take timeout from others and our routines, to reconnect with God. In the peace, and relative silence, we may hear nothing. That itself is a powerful lesson in a world that is rarely silent and always seeking our attention.

> When he opened the seventh seal, there was silence in heaven for about half an hour.
> **Revelation 8:1**

This is not just about silence from the world, silence because the TV is switched off, or you're in another room trying to pray – but absolute *silence!* It seems in this verse that the angelic worship was suspended, and even God stopped speaking. Thirty minutes

---

[225] 1 Kings 17:2-6
[226] 1 Kings 19 recounts all the details.

of silence. Not ten minutes of being alone with your thoughts, planning fantasy conversations to resolve ongoing issues, followed by ten minutes of flicking through your Bible hoping to alight upon some timely God-word, then a further ten minutes of daydreaming, checking your watch or phone to see when the thirty minutes will be up. No, none of that. Thirty minutes of silence. Not reading your Bible, I don't know about you, but my Bible is often a noisy place, with people talking, frequent battles, the waves of the sea and the public proclamations of Old Testament prophets. This isn't silent mediation, chewing over a single Bible truth for half-an-hour. Revelation 8 is silence. Set your phone's timer for 30 minutes, and quietly say, 'God I'm here. Still the world around me and be increasingly real.' Then wait for the alarm to ring.

When that happens, attempt to write down your first thoughts. Like rising from a dream, these impressions can be easily lost once the regular sounds of the world re-invade your mind. Later you can revisit those first thoughts and pray through the significance of your thirty minutes of silence.

We know that God loves us and only has the best for us, which means we can handle His silence. Silence can be like a much-needed refreshing drink in a parched land. We often live in environments filled with empty words, broken promises, exaggeration, selfishness, deception, addictions, abuse, fears and anxieties. Must I go on? In the world most of us inhabit – silence is golden, especially when your seated in the presence of the Creator and Saviour of the World.

Apart from seeking that occasional total silence, Bible mediation, as addressed earlier in the book has its merits, as we deliberately detached from life's routines, people and their needs, and the screen on our phone – which can easily become highly addictive. Sit a while with a Bible truth and hang out with God.

> Peace I [JESUS] leave with you; my peace I give you. I do not give to you as the world gives. Do not let your hearts be troubled and do not be afraid.
> **John 14:27**

> And the peace of God, which transcends all understanding, will guard your hearts and your minds in Christ Jesus.
> **Philippians 4:7**

I love Paul's words here, it's as if the learned Pharisee, now a zealous apostle is giving us a choice between, understanding and peace. Be careful, choose wisely. Don't panic. The choice often presents itself to us again – so we can have another go. At times God does show us His divine purposes to allow us a level of understanding. Though often, we need simply to trust and rest in His divine peace. A peace that soothes, refreshes, renews, cleanses, and empowers. His peace is great! Beware, there's still two trees in the garden, one that oozes life and the other so-called knowledge – choose wisely[227].

Simplicity

I believe simplicity is a by-product of solitude. The wise personal choice to take timeout leads to our refreshing, and very often a recalibrating of our lives toward the 'simplicity of Christ' as opposed to the complexity, and eventual captivity of the world.

Throughout this book, I've sought to highlight how the simple is not always easy, but that the alternative, which often seems more manageable, is actually far more time consuming and often leads to cultivating very different fruit. Here in this section, these principles can still be applied, though the concept of simplicity in this context is more pragmatic – to choose to live simply. To avoid the snares of stuff. I could write about my life of various coffee machines and the money I've invested (wasted) over the years. However, one person's enticement is just trivia to someone else. Some of you are gadget people, needing the next digital device. Perhaps your thing is branding, wearing the right clothing labels, having the right car badge, or that highly respected name at the top of your guitar's machine-head. Others of you aren't relating to this at all, then, rejoice. Though note, we don't have the phrase, *keeping up with the Jones'* for nothing. Life can be troublesome,

---

[227] This is an analogy for so many of life's choices, just like Eden, we can choose feed on life or acquire a form of knowledge. Often that knowledge leads to judgments and divisions, whereas life affirming words can bring encouragement, hope and renewed vision.

even dangerously reckless, if our eyes alight upon the wrong things.

There's also a warning here, if simplicity becomes an obsession – you've failed. Simplicity ought to create natural space for calmer living. It is not a campaign to find the next bargain, the cheapest grocery shop, or to argue with all your utility providers for better deals. Nor is it about being poor. Real poverty is exhausting and often has both physical and mental consequences.

Perhaps simplicity can only truly be pursued when you face genuine choices. Often those choices are about material things, but just as important, we have choices about our emotional energy and our use of free time. How we chose to daydream, or fret over a problem will affect our mental health. Unforgiveness is a big drain on many people's lives.

Don't let the pursuit of simplicity become a campaign for social justice. That's an entirely different matter. Simplicity is the re-ordering of your personal life to avoid unnecessary stress, personal comparisons and competition. Holistic simplicity will become a state of mind, part of your character, a freeing attribute that will make you more centred and genuine, and as a result more trustworthy and approachable.

Submission

I naturally react badly to this word. Which is probably why it's deemed a discipline. If submission is something you crave, then I have to question your understanding of the word, and even your general mindset. In my pastoral ministry, I have met people who desire to be controlled. A pseudo-submission, where they accept domination by others freeing them from needing to take personal responsibility. Sadly, some churches, rather like cults, choose to be authoritarian, twisting biblical language to manipulate unhealthy submissive behaviour. This is *not* Christian submission.

Submission begins with God, it's an act of worship[228]; as we submit, or surrender, our lives to God. We are that living sacrifice Paul talks of in Romans 12:1. The image is quite weird – a *living* sacrifice. He goes on to talk about having our minds renewed. We're not physically put to death, but we are choosing to kill areas of our lives and thoughts that are counter to God's Kingdom.

Paul immediately after telling us to be continually filled with the Holy Spirit tells us to submit to one another[229]. Submitting to others, for most of us, is not an easy option. However, once we've learnt to submit to God, allowing Him to prune our lives for greater fruit[230], we will hopefully see the value of trusting God over our own initial and selfish thoughts. Again, not necessarily easy. God may be asking you to make some significant lifestyle

---

[228] Romans 12:1
[229] Ephesians 5:17-21
[230] John 15:2-4

changes. Hence the increased need to be part of a healthy local church, where some close and trusted believers can help advise and support you.

So, you've been pruned by God. You've laid some stuff down, and hopefully the God in you is becoming more visible to others, as the 'me first' mindset is changed to 'first God'[231]. What of other Christians? Can you see the Christ in them? Sadly, not always! Nevertheless, hopefully with a healthy fellowship and good friends, you'll start to enjoy meeting together, and detecting the spiritual dimension of being together 'in Christ'. Now, as we see Christ in each other, including different giftings and abilities, submission to one another becomes a possibility. This is not about leadership, or people unjustly exercising their authority over you. This is about encountering something freeing and rewarding in submitting to the knowledge and abilities of others in order for a task to be done more efficiently and productively. For over thirty years I was either the lone pastor or senior pastor of different congregations. Yet within those roles, I happily wore different hats to help facilitate someone else's vision. It wasn't always easy, especially if I found myself outside my comfort zone, but nevertheless it's important to make yourself available to help others across the breadth of church ministry and mission.

Submission is almost logical in some environments. When flying I submit to the trained cabin crew. When in hospital, I choose to

---

[231] Luke 9:57-62, these reluctant followers have excuses that begin, *first let me.*

submit to the qualified medical team seeking to treat me. I know of people who fight against these things. I've witnessed arrogant people argue with flight attendants, and others who dismiss the advice of doctors. We probably all have some anecdotal story to counter this approach, but nine times out of ten, submission to the skills of others results in a better outcome.

Then when you submit to serve and help others, without seeking a reward or a favour in return, God sees the genuineness of your humility and (I believe) can't help but bless you. It's *not* a formula, otherwise it wouldn't be true and genuine submission, it's the result of a loving Father lavishing His affection on His willing children. Learning to submit, support and help others is a Christlike quality, for He came not to be served but to serve[232].

---

[232] Matthew 20:28, Mark 10:45 & John 13:1-17

> Discipleship is about becoming more like Jesus, discerning the work of the Father, and keeping in step with the Holy Spirit.

Discipleship is about becoming more Jesus, discerning the work of the Father, and keeping in step with the Holy Spirit. *Simple.*

Though to achieve these goals, you need to be reading the Bible, praying regularly, fellowshipping with other believers, engaging in environments of praise and prophecy, nurturing several personal disciplines and serving in both the church and across your local community. Yeah, tell me about, effective spiritual formation is not always – *easy*. But hey, **get stuck in!**

Final Remarks

The apostle Paul often ended his letters with some personal shoutouts. I feel compelled to do the same, for if there is any wisdom in these pages, the credit is not all mine, that's for sure. For those who knowingly and unknowingly shaped and enhanced my discipleship – *Thank you*.

The Gideon's movement, that back in 1975 gave me, along with the rest of my school year, a free copy of the New Testament. I can't be the only one who read it and found a Saviour?

Malcom and Alwyn, for your *Wildwall* album. Those songs contained enough truth, that they served as my initial discipleship lessons. Over forty years later I still listen to them.

SCHOOL OF DISCIPLESHIP

Mr Irvin Winson. Looking back at your generosity of time and your absolute zeal for winning new lives to Christ, modern safeguarding policies would now put strict limits on your work! Thankfully it was 1977 and you could pick me up at the end of the road and drive me to your Covenanter group. I never got a bronze or silver sword award, but I did get my initial 10 consecutive weeks badge. I also witnessed 'twenty-something' Rory, play his twelve-string acoustic guitar as he led us in simple Christian choruses. The result? I was inspired to learn the guitar and do likewise.

Steve Woolley, the young *Brummie* Baptist minister in Gloucester. You were my mentor the moment I arrived at Kendal Road Baptist Church. You gave me baptismal lessons, you baptised me, then later baptised my Mum and later again, my Dad. I still remember the sermon series you were preaching when I first arrived in July 1977. Your honest zeal for God outshone any need for clever academia. You showed me true worship, with songs that were modern, accessible and spiritually intimate. With hindsight, I know your time in Gloucester was not all plain sailing, you soon moved on down to the south coast – I was gutted, but such is life. We met again at the conference, *Leadership '89*, still passionate, still motivational, still with your *Brummie* accent!

George Verwer, international director and founder of *Operation Mobilisation*. For your books, tapes, teaching, conferences, personal example, your extraordinary and diverse leadership team and my unforgettable Gap Year – nothing can express my thanks for twelve full months of spiritual adventures in evangelism, and

FINAL REMARKS

the opportunity to exercise and develop my own leadership abilities. You guys gave me a solid foundation and an insatiable hunger for more.

London Bible College (1983-1986) – for me unforgettable, you gave me a renewed Bible, full of content I had (embarrassingly) never seen before. Dr Max Turner, you introduced me the Kingdom of God, which remains my lasting piece of revelatory teaching, which I continue to impart to others. Peggy Knight and Mary Evans gave me an eye-opening love and appreciation for the Old Testament, that remains to this day.

Neil Loxley – I first met you in September 1983, one of the first students to welcome me to London Bible College. And now it's 2024, and the rest is history. So much has happened. So many memories. So many God-orientated conversations. You and Maggie have been there in the highs and the lows – my confidantes. We even managed to work together for eight years, without messing up our friendship. As I write this, we called each other less than two weeks ago – that's true friendship.

Jane Rennie (1964-2004), my first wife. She grounded our shared academia into an efficient and profound spirituality. Lessons learnt I've never forgotten. Obviously, there's more to say, but it's getting a little too personal. So, forgive my heavy editing and redactions from this point on.

SCHOOL OF DISCIPLESHIP

As I attempt to close, there are a few more additional shoutouts, some of whom I only saw at a distance, yet all remain inspirational in continuing to form my discipleship.

- John Wimber, for your own extraordinary testimony and the international ministry that followed. Since you first laid hands on me and prayed for me in 1985 and everything since; your Bible teaching and worship insights have been one of the most influential in shaping my own approach to public ministry, prayer ministry, deliverance ministry and corporate praise.
- Roger and Sue Mitchell, for resharpening my radical edge, for helping to facilitate such closeness to the celestial courts, which brought timeless insights into the spiritual realm. Thank for the privilege of hanging out with you and many of your ministry friends, Ed Silvoso, Martin Scott, Victor Lorenzo and Dr Paul Cox.
- Bill Johnson and your team. I'm grieved that the dawning of the Internet has allowed controversy and lies to abound. Nevertheless, your words, insights and ministry and those of your closest colleagues and ministry friends have never let me down. From a distance, you impart faith and stimulate motivation for greater spiritual living.
- Teresa Lasky, for showing me how intercession is both apostolic and prophetic. For the hours of laughter in His presence, for the crazy breaker-anointed visions and shared prophetic ministry. You're a one-off, an original, and

FINAL REMARKS

a dearly missed friend as geography continues to separate us.
- Bernie and Margaret Andrew – co-workers in the Kingdom and such supportive friends. I long for the next time we meet, for I know there will be godly tears, and many others will be blessed through your faithfulness and fearlessness. While we are apart, stay sharp, stay strong and stay influential.
- David Haussmann and your beautiful family. Since the last century you've been a positive presence in my life. You have had such faith in me and given me great opportunities to minister, and now, like a spiritual son or older brother, you have your own stories of God's goodness and faithfulness. For you, and for Alain and Ann, *glug, glug, glug,* such treasured memories, such laughter, such a good good God.
- Then finally, like the writer to the Hebrews at the close of chapter 11, what of all the others? We haven't time to mention Gideon – poor Gideon, almost made the list.
    - The prophetic words from ministering strangers, whose names I can't even remember. Such as the Egyptian prophet I met in France, who first encouraged me to write a book, against all my fears, linked to my past disabilities with language.
    - The Jordanian believer who spent the night sharing a number of his life stories with us youngsters as we crowded round a dining-room table in a suburban house in West London. An unforgettable night with

- a forgotten-named hero who completely oozed Jesus.
  - All the positivity of people responding to God's presence in various times of ministry. Thank you, watching *you* get blessed, both blessed and encouraged *me*.
  - Vanessa, for being so teachable, a spiritual sponge, you soaked it in, and then with your own confident leadership skills, squeezed it all out again onto others, generation to generation… now that's what I call effective Christian discipleship!

Last but not least! Dora Maria, my gracious wife. For being a fearless evangelist, a faithful intercessor and a true lover of God. Your spirituality seeps into my being and makes me long for more of God at every spiritual level and across every ministry. Words alone can't express my thanks for your example and instructions.

Well, that's my incomplete list of discipleship heroes who have shaped my spirituality. Time now for you to begin compiling your own list, and applying this humble book to your life.

I pray, that 'in Christ Jesus' and through His Holy Spirit, you will mature, grow in faith, become a positive Kingdom influencer and an outrageous lover of God. Amen.